STEP INTO THE WATER

An Invitation to Deepen Your Relationship with the Holy Spirit of God

PEG RANKIN

D0168675

Renew

A Division of Gospel Light
Ventura, California, U.S.A.

Published by Renew Books
A Division of Gospel Light
Ventura, California, U.S.A.
Printed in U.S.A.

Renew Books is a ministry of Gospel Light, an evangelical Christian publisher dedicated to serving the local church. We believe God's vision for Gospel Light is to provide church leaders with
biblical, user-friendly materials that will help them evangelize, disciple and minister to children,
youth and families.

It is our prayer that this Renew book will help you discover biblical truth for your own life and
help you meet the needs of others. May God richly bless you.

For a free catalog of resources from Renew Books/Gospel Light please contact your Christian
supplier or call 1-800-4-GOSPEL.

Cover Design by Barbara LeVan Fisher
Interior Design by Britt Rocchio
Edited by Virginia Woodard

Library of Congress Cataloging-in-Publication Data
Rankin, Peg.
    Step into the water : an invitation to deepen your relationship with the Holy Spirit of God / Peg
Rankin.
        p. cm.
    Includes bibliographical references.
    ISBN 0-8307-2145-2 (trade paper)
    1. Holy Spirit. 2. Spiritual life—Christianity. I. Title.
    BT121.2.R36 1998
    248.4—dc21   97-43798
                                                                                      CIP

1 2 3 4 5 6 7 8 9 10 11 12 13 14 15 16 17 18 19 20 / 04 03 02 01 00 99 98

Rights for publishing this book in other languages are contracted by Gospel Literature International
(GLINT). GLINT also provides technical help for the adaptation, translation and publishing of Bible
study resources and books in scores of languages worldwide. For further information, contact GLINT,
P.O. Box 4060, Ontario, CA 91761-1003, U.S.A., or the publisher.

praise for STEP INTO THE WATER

God is beckoning His people to experience His
refreshing and renewing touch. Peg Rankin's natural,
easy writing style helps us enter into God's presence,
the place from which His living water flows.

JANE HANSEN
INTERNATIONAL PRESIDENT, AGLOW INTERNATIONAL
EDMONDS, WASHINGTON

"Step into the Water" is a rich, extremely personal
resource for understanding the Holy Spirit. I was
profoundly affected. I do not believe you can
read this book and remain unchanged.

PATSY CLAIRMONT
AUTHOR OF "SPORTIN' A 'TUDE" AND
"TEA WITH PATSY CLAIRMONT"
BRIGHTON, MICHIGAN

Few books have the distinction of being deeply spiritual
yet intensely practical. You'll agree "Step into the Water"
is both. With tremendous insight and remarkable clarity,
Peg Rankin shows us the way to healing, refreshing and
revival in the presence of God. With so much emphasis
on methods and formulas in today's Church, it is
encouraging to be able to recommend a book that steers
us back to the core issue—relationship with the Father.
This book will make a difference in your life!

DUTCH SHEETS
SENIOR PASTOR, SPRINGS HARVEST FELLOWSHIP
COLORADO SPRINGS, COLORADO

praise for STEP INTO THE WATER

Peg Rankin inspires and encourages us not only to experience the wonder of the Holy Spirit in our lives, but to "dive for His treasures." Drenched in scriptural truths, "Step into the Water" is an important book for old and new believers alike.

CAROLE MAYHALL
AUTHOR, SPEAKER AND HOMEMAKER
COLORADO SPRINGS, COLORADO

Who among us doesn't need a cool drink of refreshing encouragement for the soul? "Step into the Water" will quench the thirst of dry disciples and make each of us a blessing to others.

JILL BRISCOE
AUTHOR AND SPEAKER
BROOKFIELD, WISCONSIN

Poignant. Biblical. Relevant. Every Christian needs this extraordinary book. Peg Rankin has skillfully woven eternal truth with practical application to create a powerful tool that will change your life!

CAROL KENT
AUTHOR OF "TAME YOUR FEARS"
PORT HURON, MICHIGAN

This book is dedicated to
the late Reverend George H. Slavin,
who creatively revealed to me
the wonders of Ezekiel's river
that flows from the throne of God.

WITH THANKS

- to Janis Whipple for putting the project into motion
- to my husband, Lee, for enthusiastically supporting me with his advice, his computer expertise and his incredible patience (I love you!)
- to my son Jeff and his wife, Kyra, for helping with the structure of the outline and the development of the water analogy
- to my pastor, Dr. Jonathan H. Bosse, for being a ready consultant in the areas of language (Hebrew and Greek translation), as well as theological and biblical accuracy (a big job!)
- to my friend El Stewart for enriching the book with her experiences as a swimming instructor
- to my friend and mentor Eleanor Barzler for contributing gems of wisdom from her knowledge of literature and hymns, as well as the Bible
- to my sister Polly Cronin and my friends Connie Lee Bosse and Joan Sims for helping with clarity of expression, grammar and punctuation
- to my son Dirk and his wife, Laurie, for helping me construct the chapter about their son's miraculous healing
- to Margee Newell and the Reverend Stanley Rockafellow for allowing me to use their stories
- to the team at Renew Books, especially Kyle Duncan, Virginia Woodard and Gloria Moss, for working diligently with me not only to produce a book that would glorify God, but also to distribute that book to the widest possible readership
- and to all my family members and friends who prayed me through the writing process.

I am grateful!

Contents

~~~~~~

INTRODUCTION   11

"It is easy to identify with water. Its similarities to God and His Spirit are remarkable. Although water is one in substance, it has a threefold aspect. It exists as liquid, solid and gas."

PROLOGUE: A PROVOCATIVE ILLUSTRATION   15

"Permit me,...to take you to [Ezekiel's visionary] river. Experience being immersed in God's Spirit."

PART ONE:
A Personal Inventory

~~~~

1. PARCHED GROUND   23

"The Lord Jesus Christ...is the only One who can unleash the flow of His Spirit."

2. MEETING THE HELPER   31

"The Spirit,...[is] Someone who possesses an intellect, emotions and a will. We are talking about Someone to be referred to as a 'He,' not an 'It.' Jesus calls Him our 'Helper.'"

3. CLOUDBURSTS OF BLESSING   41

"When Jesus poured out His Spirit on His disciples, He poured out His very own power."

4. A REASON TO FEAR   51

"'The remarkable thing about fearing God is that when you fear God, you fear nothing else, whereas if you do not fear God, you fear everything else.'"

5. A HOLY BOLDNESS   61
"You are to worship [God] in a way that honors His transcendent holiness, yet embraces the warmth of His personal presence."

6. A FITTING LIFESTYLE   71
"'The work of the Holy Spirit is to produce a holy spirit.'"

PART TWO:
A Progressive Immersion

7. COVERING THE FEET (OUR CHRISTIAN WALK)   81
"Your driving instructor told you to STOP, LOOK, LISTEN, then GO! The same directions apply when you come to a spiritual decision point."

8. COVERING THE KNEES (OUR PRAYER LIFE)   91
"Instead of thinking of prayer as a human attempt to persuade God to do our will, think of it as God burdening His people to accomplish His will."

9. UP TO THE WAIST (REPRODUCING OUR FAITH)   101
"God...is the One who has the ability to break down barriers, cut through religiosity and soften hard hearts. The only One. The whole salvation process is His, and each Person in the Trinity is involved."

10. ENVELOPING THE HEART (OUR HIDDEN DESIRES)   111
"Heart trouble seems to be a universal disease. In the providence of God, there is hope."

11. OVER THE HEAD (OUR CONTROL CENTER)? NO!   121
"Our Christian identity lies in [Jesus Christ]. As long as He is directing the course of our lives, and we are acting in accordance with His commands, it is easy for others to recognize us as Christians."

PART THREE:
Practical Issues

12. SURRENDER! WHAT IF I CAN'T?   133
    "To believe in God,...one must have faith. Yet to have faith, one
    must believe in God. It seems like an impossible hurdle,...yet
    daily, people place their trust in their Creator."

13. WHERE DO I GO FOR HELP?   143
    "Take time to dwell 'at the footstool of the throne of God.'"

14. HERE GOES! I'M TAKING THE PLUNGE   153
    "Six steps are involved in taking the plunge: position yourself;
    present yourself; proceed forward; praise God as you go; plunge
    in; pause to reflect."

PART FOUR:
Profound Implications

15. FROM A TRICKLE TO A TORRENT   165
    "When it comes to spiritual rivers, everybody gets caught up in
    one or another....let it be *the* river, God's river."

16. TREASURES IN THE SAND   175
    "'There are deep things of God,...mysteries, hidden things,...they
    defy the wise and prudent of the world. But they are revealed to
    babes...through the grace of the Holy Spirit.'"

17. FULL NETS   185
    "[The disciples] stopped relying on themselves and started to rely
    on Someone standing on the shore;...To be successful, though,
    they had to look to Him, listen to Him and obey Him. When
    they did, they caught fish."

18. FRUIT FOR ALL SEASONS   195

"This fruit [is] called the fruit of the Spirit and not the fruit of the Christian...because the Christian is not the one who produces it. Only the Holy Spirit can produce it. It is *His* fruit."

19. NO MORE BITTERNESS   205

"If we do not forgive others, we cannot really participate in the blessings of God's forgiveness of us. Only when we let God's pardon continue its flow right on through us are we set free."

20. A HEALING TOUCH   215

"God doesn't heal every person who asks. All Christians, however, will ultimately be healed in heaven."

EPILOGUE   225

"*It will be exciting to introduce people to all the river has to offer.*"

STUDY GUIDE   229

Introduction

Oswald Chambers, the devotional writer, said, "The author who benefits you most is not the one who tells you something you did not know before, but the one who gives expression to the truth that has been dumbly struggling in you for utterance."[1] I want to be that kind of author, presenting old truths in fresh ways. I want you to read this book and say, "Wow! That's exactly how it is."

Why did I write about the third Person of the Godhead? As a Christian conference speaker with years of experience, I have observed firsthand God's people and their needs. Most long for a more vibrant faith. The Holy Spirit is the answer to their longing.

To me the Spirit is also a special Friend. Personally, I owe everything to Him. It was He who formed me in my mother's womb, then "birthed" me. It was He who introduced me to the Savior, then "rebirthed" me. It was He who thrust me out of the security of my nest and equipped me to "fly." Now it is He who moves within me day by day, nudging me here, urging me there.

We have had some thrilling experiences together, the Holy Spirit and I, especially during my devotional times. When I am reading His Correspondence, He causes me to discover things I would not otherwise see. Sometimes, He takes my random thoughts and organizes them. Occasionally, He "presses a button" that only He knows about, and relevant Scripture verses I am acquainted with but am not thinking about suddenly pop into my head. It is fun to commit my study time to Him and watch Him do "His thing."

I also appreciate the Spirit's activity when I am on the speaker's platform. Sometimes He descends so powerfully that He "electrifies me," causing the tiny hairs in my pores to rise. (Fortunately, the hairs on my head have so far remained in place.) Other times, members of the audience mention how blessed they are by something they heard me say (but I know the Voice was not mine because I never said what they thought I said). Several times people have commented favorably about something I did say but had not planned to; it just "came out." Traveling with God's Spirit is quite an adventure.

Sometimes this Helper of mine performs in a truly extraordinary way, causing me to catch my breath. At one conference when the message ended, He so paralyzed the audience that they could not move—or did not want to—for what seemed like an eternity. At another, He convicted the listeners so powerfully that the following session had to be delayed as people lined up in record numbers to symbolically place their lives and/or their burdens in the "hands" of Jesus Christ. Once, right in the middle of my message, a woman shouted, "I'm filled to overflowing." The biggest thrill of all, though, occurred the day the Spirit performed an "eye-popping miracle" in our family—a miracle you can read about later in this book.

When I started enumerating these events and dozens like them—events I attribute to the Holy Spirit—I could not contain my praise. I knew I had to share it. In the process of doing so, I realized the Spirit is not finished with me yet. More blessings are yet to come. No matter where we are in our spiritual journeys, more is always waiting ahead.

To help readers experience some of the "more," I have selected water to represent the Spirit. Why? Although the Scriptures introduce Him in other ways as well (a dove, oil, fire and wind), it is easy to identify with water. After all, it is something we use every day. Furthermore, its similarities to God and His Spirit are remarkable.

First, although water is one in substance, it has a threefold aspect. It exists as liquid, solid and gas. Second, it is essential for life and growth. Third, it has a curious "omnipresence" you can't escape. Fourth, a seemingly inexhaustible supply constantly recycles itself to wherever it is needed. Fifth, water has the unique ability to refresh, revive, purify, cleanse, support and energize. As if these were not enough reasons to support my decision, I offer one more. God chose water to unlock the mysteries of His Spirit for me personally—an experience you will read about in the prologue of this book.

Now, what do I intend for you to experience as you read? I want your heart to beat with mine, for this is a heart-to-heart book. Not that my writing isn't "theological"; I have taken pains to make sure it is doctrinally correct. Not that my words aren't applicable to life; I want them to be. Primarily, however, this work is something to be experienced. Let it become "virtual reality" to you. Get "into it."

Start now. Enter God's throne room and feel your heart leap into your throat as you realize you are standing in the presence of the One who created you. Let Him point out the beginning of His "river" of life. Follow the trickle as it increases in volume. Come close. Marvel at its beauty. Touch its coolness. Splash your arms. Listen to the gurgle. Breathe in deeply. Taste the river's purity. React. Become involved. Get caught up in what is happening. As you do, worship. Worship the Father. Worship the Son. Worship the Holy Spirit. Experience being in the very presence of God.

Note
1. Oswald Chambers, *My Utmost for His Highest* (New York: Dodd, Mead, and Company, 1935), p. 350.

Prologue:
A Provocative Illustration

THE RIVER FROM THE TEMPLE

The man brought me back to the entrance of the temple, and I saw water coming out from under the threshold of the temple toward the east (for the temple faced east). The water was coming down from under the south side of the temple, south of the altar. He then brought me out through the north gate and led me around the outside to the outer gate facing east, and the water was flowing from the south side.

As the man went eastward with a measuring line in his hand, he measured off a thousand cubits and then led me through water that was ankle-deep. He measured off another thousand cubits and led me through water that was knee-deep. He measured off another thousand and led me through water that was up to the waist. He measured off another thousand, but now it was a river that I could not cross, because the water had risen and was deep enough to swim in—a river that no one could cross. He asked me, "Son of man, do you see this?"

Then he led me back to the bank of the river. When I arrived there, I saw a great number of trees on each side of the river. He said to me, "This water flows toward the eastern region and goes down into the Arabah, where it enters the Sea. When it empties into the Sea, the water there becomes fresh. Swarms of living creatures will live wherever the river flows. There will be large numbers of fish, because this water flows there and makes the salt water fresh; so where the river flows everything will live. Fishermen will stand along the shore; from En Gedi to En Eglaim there will be places for spreading nets. The fish will be of many kinds—like the fish of the Great Sea.

"But the swamps and marshes will not become fresh; they will be left for salt. Fruit trees of all kinds will grow on both banks of the river. Their leaves will not wither, nor will their fruit fail. Every month they will bear, because the water from the sanctuary flows to them. Their fruit will serve for food and their leaves for healing" (Ezek. 47:1-12).

One Sunday morning years ago, our beloved pastor, George Slavin, preached powerfully from Ezekiel 47:1-12, the text cited above. Exactly what he said that morning I cannot recall.

What the Holy Spirit showed me, though, as He applied the imagery of the water to Himself, the "man" to a more mature Christian, and the hesitant bather to me, I will never forget. Although physically I was sitting in a church pew, spiritually I was in Ezekiel's sandals, standing by his visionary river, observing its emergence from the throne of God.

Permit me, if you will, to take you to that river. Stand where I stood. Feel what I felt. Experience being immersed in God's Spirit.

Imagine you are standing in the sand beside a wide body of running water. The day is sultry, so you are dressed in shorts, a top and sandals.

Lining the water's edge are trees that provide shade from the sweltering heat, but they are farther up the sloping bank. Where you are standing, only sun and water and the blazing reflection of one upon the other are visible. You shield your eyes.

The water is calm near the river's edge. Its gentle waves are lapping up the beach. Children are carrying buckets and shovels to a shallow pool. There they wade, splash and play, expressing squeals of delight. You catch yourself smiling.

Farther up the beach, fishermen are casting lines. Every once in a while one reels in a catch. The rest offer their approval. They seem to enjoy encouraging each other. *What support!* you think.

In a spot set aside for swimmers, much activity is taking place. You enjoy watching attempts at the crawl, the butterfly, the sidestroke and more. Every movement appears effortless. You conclude, though, that that is only because the swimmers know what they are doing. Swimming would not be so easy for you.

While you are contemplating your own shortcomings, a swimmer dives beneath the surface. When he emerges, he is holding up something.

"Look what I found!" he shouts.

His enthusiasm is a magnet. Soon many swimmers are also displaying "treasures." You are envious.

Way out, where the river is deepest, the current is running swiftly. Those who choose to venture that far are not actually "swimming." They just seem to be going with the flow, relishing every minute of the ride.

That is not for you, though. You are afraid of water. Oh, you love its beauty, you love its sound and you love to feel its mist on your bare skin; but that is the extent of your involvement with water. You are a spectator, not a participant. At least that has been your thinking until now.

From the deepest part of the river you notice a man swimming toward you. When he gets closer, he stands up. Then he splashes his way to the beach. He looks as if he would like to strike up a conversation. You wait.

"Come on in," he invites in a friendly tone. "The water's great."

"No thanks," you answer. "I can't swim."

"No problem," the stranger counters. "I'll teach you."

"I'm not sure I want to learn," you protest.

"That's too bad," he comments. "You're missing a thrill."

"That's what I've heard."

"Then why don't you try it?" He points to a spot in the shallows. "Here. Take off your sandals and step in right here."

You obey, cautiously touching your toes to the wetness.

You draw back quickly. "It's cold."

"It does seem that way at first," your mentor assures you. "But the longer you are in it, the more accustomed you will become. Try again."

You do, letting the water cover your feet. You feel its gentle motion as it laps around your ankles. You press your toes into the moist sand—not a bad sensation.

You look up. Your guide has moved backward a few steps. He is beckoning again. "Let the water cover your knees."

Hesitantly you move forward. You notice he is smiling.

"Slowly now," he advises. Then he urges, "Keep coming." You are watching him as he continues to back up.

He's out too far, you say to yourself. What seems dangerous to you, though, does not seem to be fazing him at all. Then you remember. He is familiar with the deep part. He came from there.

"Move farther out," he encourages. "You'll like the feel of the current."

Maybe I will, you think as you push your legs forward. Soon you are submerged up to the waist. Pressing against the weight of the water is quite a struggle now. You also note, feeling some trepidation, how hard it is to keep your feet on the bottom. Then, too, you have the odd sensation you are disappearing, more and more with every step you take.

You glance toward your instructor. He looks as if he is in over his head, but a casual observer would never know it. He is treading water effortlessly.

As he is moving backward, you are advancing. Suddenly you realize you are in up to your neck.

"This is as far as I go," you announce, as the water touches your ears.

Then you hear your mentor say, "Don't stop now. Continue to come."

"I can't," you try to explain. "I will drown."

"No you won't," he reassures you. "You will learn to swim. But to do so, you must let the water cover your head. Don't worry about the consequences. I'm here. I won't let anything bad happen."

Can you trust this man? This is heavy stuff. You realize you are at a crossroads. You must either go back to the beach and continue to sweat out a mediocre existence, or take a refreshing risk and experience all God has in store for you.

You decide to risk it, no holds barred.

"Here's goes nothing!" you shout, before you have a chance to change your mind. Then quickly you shut your eyes, hold your nose and go under.

Help! My feet have left the bottom, you are thinking; *they're flailing wildly. I can't hold my breath. I'm going to drown. I know it. I must regain control. I'm thrashing around like a madman.*

Finally your head breaks the surface. *Air! I'm alive.* Your coach is there, right beside you. "Lean back," he advises, as he places a hand underneath you. "Give up the struggle. Let the water support you. It will—if you just give it a chance."

You know you are tense. You can't seem to help it. So you concentrate on relaxing. It is a muscle-by-muscle exercise in mental discipline. *Let go*, you tell yourself. *Give up. Surrender. Trust the water. There now....*

Ah! It's working. You are not sure when or how it happened, but in a moment, in a flash, your fear turned into faith. Not an I'm-ready-to-go-all-the-way faith, but faith nonetheless. Excitement wells up within you.

"Hey, I'm floating," you inform your guide.

"I know," he smiles, gradually withdrawing support. "The water is holding you up. Before long you'll be swimming—then diving—and bringing up treasure with the best of them."

Reader, wouldn't it be wonderful if this swimming guide's prediction proved true? That in the course of time you became trusting enough not only to venture into deeper spiritual truth, but also to let God's current carry you there? Wouldn't it be thrilling if you found yourself in the middle of somebody's desert, offering a cup of cold water in your Savior's name? Or if you were transported to a fishing area and could catch a few souls? Or if you traveled close enough to the banks to pluck fruit of the Spirit from trees whose boughs hang heavy?

Wouldn't it be exciting to watch people come to this river of life, some for fruit, some for leaves, some to fish, some to fill up their jugs, some to picnic and some to swim?

What if you were privileged to be THEIR instructor?

Come now, wouldn't that be wonderful?

PART ONE:
A Personal Inventory

Examine yourselves to see whether
you are in the faith; test yourselves.
2 Corinthians 13:5

1

Parched Ground

～～～～

"The poor and needy search for water, but there is none;
their tongues are parched with thirst. But I the Lord will
answer them;...I will make rivers flow on barren heights,
and springs within the valleys. I will turn the desert into
pools of water, and the parched ground into springs."

ISAIAH 41:17,18

Having grown up on a farm, I know the meaning of the word "drought."
I remember the day I first noticed how hot the sun could be. As I ran
from its glare, it occurred to me it had been beating down like that for
weeks, and no relief was in sight. Our fields were fading, and our crops
were beginning to wilt. In places, the earth was cracking and separating
into chunks as hard as stone. What to do?

I suggested running for a watering can and saving as many plants as I
could, but that would be an effort in futility, Daddy said. Tough words to
a little girl of eight who loved to watch things grow.

At one point during that summer, Daddy gathered our family around
the kitchen table and made a pronouncement. "It's going to be a bleak
winter," he said. We knew what he meant. No rain, no harvest. No harvest, no food. Like the plants I had yearned to salvage, we would be struggling to survive.

The struggle never came, at least from my perspective. Why, I am not sure. Maybe when I was not looking, the Lord multiplied our "loaves and fishes." Or perhaps my parents were very good stewards, stretching what we had effectively. It could have been a combination of both. Whatever it was, it did not affect me.

I do, however, remember accompanying my father to the woods on our property for more hunting trips than usual. There he shot rabbits and squirrels for dinner. I have a mental picture of Mother cooking the critters whole, then serving them, legs up, on a platter. (This is probably why I politely refuse such "gourmet fare" today; I just can't get those legs out of my mind.) Our dinners were nutritious and filling, though. No bleak winter for me.

Back to that long, hot summer. One day the sky sported some dark clouds. To me clouds meant hope, and I wanted to be the first to see that hope become reality. So I ran outside, looked heavenward and waited.

Splat! Splat! Splat! Huge drops began descending from above. I watched as they made patterns in the dusty earth. Then I ran inside. "Rain!" I announced. "Rain!"

I raced to the window, flattened my nose to the pane and marveled as God displayed more of His handiwork. Droplets were snuggling into the base of leaves, then spilling over, rinsing away dirt that had been accumulating for weeks. Droopy shrubs were beginning to revive, right before my eyes. How exciting to watch this refreshment from heaven!

It was a treat for the ears, too. I sprinted upstairs and, as hot as it was, slid under my quilt, bunched it around my neck and listened. Patter, patter, patter came the gentle sound upon the roof. It made me feel cozy and safe—and very, very special. You see, God was answering my prayers.

After receiving Mother's permission I was soon back outside, minus my shoes and socks. What fun to splash around in the puddles! What a sensation to hold my arms out monster style and feel water dripping from my fingertips! I did not care that my hair was getting soaked. Nor did I give a thought to my sunsuit becoming soggier by the minute. It was raining, and I was having an experience.

Now I am grown. Through the years have come rain hats, raincoats, umbrellas and boots—and a decided reluctance to let showers touch me. I have asked myself why—why this reticence among some adults to get wet? Are we so busy taking videos of life and watching them play on a screen that we have forgotten how much fun it is to experience life firsthand? Or is it that we now have an image to protect? Maybe we have all turned into sunbathers—no rain allowed in our daily routine. Or perhaps we are afraid of what the rain might do. Whatever the reason, we are missing a blessing. I would like to see us get it back—physically, yes. Spiritually, for sure!

RAIN ON ME, LORD!

Like the fields on my father's farm, many Christians are experiencing drought. John MacArthur, a pastor-teacher, says, "The tragedy in so many Christian lives is not the tragedy of living horribly immoral lives, it's the tragedy of living disastrously inconsequential lives."[1] Reading those words, you might think we are lazy about demonstrating our faith. On the contrary, we are running to church every time the doors are open.

We are teaching Sunday School, singing in the choir, serving on committees, participating in Bible studies, attending men's and women's functions and reading our daily devotionals. We are faithfully entering our prayer closets, paying tribute to the good Lord whenever we have a chance and even memorizing a Scripture verse or two. We sometimes do these things for God, however, rather than letting His Spirit do them through us. The result is lifeless Christianity.

> YOUR "doing" may have become
> a substitute for HIS "doing."

How about you? Do you find yourself attending church but not necessarily worshiping God? Teaching the Scriptures without deepening your relationship with the Author? Serving on committees only out of obligation? Saying your prayers but feeling you have not connected? Wanting to share your faith but not knowing where to start? Memorizing verses but not assimilating their meaning? Reading the Bible but not hearing the Spirit's voice? Singing God's praises but missing His power?

YOUR "doing" may have become a substitute for HIS "doing." Thus you are feeling the loss. You are going through a religious ritual, but your soul is experiencing a vacuum. You are in a desert, and deserts can be lonely. You are seeking water, but where is the oasis? Even if you know its location, you do not have time to go there. Or because of your religious tradition, you are reluctant. Then there is the problem of pride: *What will people think if they see me stooping to drink from God's well? It'll look like everything I've been doing up until now doesn't count!*

> The flow of God's Spirit,
> which is more action than
> activities, is not generated by
> us. It is generated by Him.

How to handle this tension? You are nagged by questions, plagued with doubts, hounded by uncertainties and forced to keep on doing religion the world's way. A. W. Tozer, an author-pastor, sums up our plight by writing these words: "Most of us go through life praying a little, planning a little, jockeying for position, hoping but never quite certain of anything, and always secretly afraid we will miss the way."[2] What a predicament!

WHERE DOES OUR PROBLEM ORIGINATE?

Our problem originates with us. We are caught up in a flow of activity, but Jesus Christ is not its Author, not of our projects that are "Christian," not of our deeds performed for Him. Jesus taught that on the Day of Judgment many will testify to prophesying, driving out demons and performing miracles—all in His name—and He will say to them, "I never knew you"[3] (perhaps because they never really knew Him). To know Him is what eternal life is all about.[4]

In contrast, the flow of God's Spirit, which is more action than activities, is not generated by us. It is generated by Him. It issues from His throne. To benefit from it, we must acknowledge, receive and submit to Jesus Christ as Lord of our lives.

Watchman Nee, the Chinese preacher, reminds us, "Not until the Lordship of Christ in our hearts is a settled thing, can the Spirit really operate effectively in us. If we do not give Him absolute authority there, He can be present, but He cannot be powerful. The power of the Spirit is stayed."[5] Of course it is.

When we try to live the Christian life on our own, we dam up the flow of the Spirit. Not only that, we usurp authority that is not ours. It is, however, an empty authority, for it has no power. Just as my father could not make it rain on his parched fields, so we cannot alleviate our spiritual drought. Oh, we try. We shout our frustration to the skies, gather fellow Christians to plan and perform our "rain dances" and hire experts to "seed our clouds"—all in an effort to produce a refreshing change. Until God shouts, "Rain!" however, the windows of heaven will remain locked.

It has been said, "In every heart there is a cross and a throne. And those upon them must change places." So to all of us a question presents itself: Who is on the throne of our lives? Are we relegating Christ to the position of victim and claiming His seat for ourselves? How are we doing in this position of control? Putting forth lots of effort, but powerless to change lives, including our own? Why don't we turn to the One who can? To the One who rose from the dead, ascended to His Father's throne and is seated at His right hand even now, full of power and glory?

Jesus Christ is no longer nailed to the cross. That spot is reserved for us. We are the ones whose turn it is to make a sacrifice, a "living sacrifice" in our case, a sacrifice of our "bodies" (see Rom. 12:1). As we dedicate our minds, eyes, ears, mouths, hearts, hands, knees and feet to the Lord, we are giving up control of them. We are climbing onto "the tree" and dying to Self.

The sacrifice is worth it. For from calvary, and only from calvary, do we have a true view of the throne and the One who sits upon it.

Once Self submits to the Father and Jesus Christ is acknowledged as Lord, something happens in heaven. Bam! The windows of blessing open, and out pours a virtual flood of love and grace. It makes us wonder why we waited so long for God's "anointing," doesn't it?

WHO DOES THE POURING?

The Lord Jesus Christ does the pouring. He is the only One who can unleash the flow of His Spirit. He is also the perfect One to do so. After all, He knows all about deserts and their heat. He spent time in them Himself, not only in physical deserts, but in spiritual ones as well. As He wandered through the wilderness of Judea, He also languished in the wasteland of loneliness, misunderstanding, rejection and pain. Because He identified with our world of struggle, we can identify with His world of victory. All of us can. Not one of us needs to be left out.

"The river of God, which is full of water," the British evangelist, F. B. Meyer, says, "flows from the threshold of [Jesus'] humanity, that it may be within the reach of the weakest and smallest in His kingdom."[6] No matter what our need, we can all be included in God's plan.

It is a plan that involves not only people, but circumstances as well, including spiritual drought. Feeling drained can result in redemptive purposes. It both gives an appreciation for what really matters and enables the one who is thirsty to empathize with other thirsty people.

"Can he who hath never thirsted know the preciousness of water?" Amy Carmichael, missionary-author, asks. "Can he who hath not found rivers on bare heights lead his fellow to those rivers? Can he who hath not walked in the deep valleys of the Spirit help the fainting find fountains? Can he who hath never seen the glowing sand become a pool bear witness to the marvel of God's power?"[7]

Andrew Murray confirms, "It is only unto the thirst of an empty soul that the streams of living water flow." Then he adds, "Ever thirsting is the secret of never thirsting."[8]

To ever thirst for God. To be fulfilled and unfulfilled, both at the same time. What a challenging paradox!

"O God," A. W. Tozer exclaims, "I have tasted Thy goodness, and it has both satisfied me and made me thirsty for more. I am painfully conscious of my need for further grace. I am ashamed of my lack of desire. O God, the Triune God, I do want to want Thee; I long to be filled with longing; I thirst to be made more thirsty still."[9]

COME AND DRINK

Only One can satisfy a yearning soul. A woman from Samaria found this out. Drawing water from a well in the heat of the day, she was forced to admit the ways of the world could not fulfill her. She was lacking something. Then she met Him: Jesus. She heard Him say as He pointed to the well, "'Everyone who drinks this water will be thirsty again, but whoever drinks the water I give him will never thirst. Indeed, the water I give him will become in him a spring of water welling up to eternal life.'"[10]

The woman drank the water Jesus offered and her thirst was quenched. When she offered water to her friends, they, too, were satisfied. They all followed Jesus for "more." The water that flows from the throne of God not only quenches thirst, but has "drawing" power as well.

It invites all of us to drink. "The wilderness life is not destined to be our perpetual experience," F. B. Meyer says. Rather, "we are bidden to come up from it."[11] Yes, we are. Our Lord extends a personal invitation: "'Come, all you who are thirsty, come to the waters.'"[12]

What He seems to be saying is, "Approach My throne. Turn over the reins of your life. Stop trying to impress Me with your religiosity. Admit your need, and I will fill you. And you will overflow. This does not mean that your life will suddenly become problem free or that you will turn into a spiritual giant overnight. But it does mean that you will have Someone to carry your burdens, Someone to take your hand and lead the way, Someone to hold you close when you feel overwhelmed and Someone you can know intimately and powerfully. But you must come to the water. Come now."

What will your answer be? If it is what I am hoping it will be, you better get ready. For a cloudburst is in the making. God is about to shout, "Rain!"

Notes

1. John MacArthur, *The Second Coming of the Lord Jesus Christ* (Panorama City, Calif.: Word of Grace Communications, 1981), p. 92.
2. A. W. Tozer, *The Knowledge of the Holy* (New York: HarperCollins, 1961), p. 69.
3. Matthew 7:23.
4. See John 17:3.
5. Watchman Nee, *The Normal Christian Life* (Fort Washington, Pa.: Christian Literature Crusade, 1963), p. 97.
6. F. B. Meyer, *Daily Meditations* (Dallas, Tex.: Word Books, 1979), September 27.
7. Amy Carmichael, *His Thoughts Said, His Father Said*, ed. Al Bryant (Fort Washington, Pa.: Christian Literature Crusade, 1993), p. 26.
8. Andrew Murray, *Abide in Christ* (Fort Washington, Pa.: Christian Literature Crusade, 1968), p. 96.
9. A. W. Tozer, *The Pursuit of God* (Harrisburg, Pa.: Christian Publications, Inc., 1948), p. 20.
10. John 4:13,14.
11. F. B. Meyer, *Daily Meditations*, July 16.
12. Isaiah 55:1.

Meeting the Helper

~~~~~~~

"When the Helper comes, whom I will send to you
from the Father, that is the Spirit of truth, who proceeds
from the Father, He will bear witness of Me."
JOHN 15:26 *(NASB)*

Did you ever wonder what people in the days before the Great Flood must have thought when they saw the first raindrops? According to some Bible commentators, up till Noah's time the earth had been watered by mists. So although God had predicted "rain" and the patriarch had built an ark in preparation, the people may have been mystified when water started falling from heaven.

We experience a similar bewilderment today when we witness the incredible abilities of water. This liquid, which appears to be so "limp" when viewed in a glass, when unleashed on the landscape can chisel rocks, carve canyons, redeposit topsoil and actually transfigure the earth. How does it do so? We do not know. We are given scientific explanations and we still have questions. It appears God reserves total understanding of natural phenomena for Himself.

It is the same with supernatural phenomena, such as the workings of the Spirit. Here we also encounter a mystery. In comparing the actions of the Spirit to wind, Jesus said, "[It] blows wherever it pleases. You hear its sound, but you cannot tell where it comes from or where it is going."[1] The Spirit's workings leave us wondering.

When Jesus Christ tabernacled on earth, people had questions about Him, too. Who was He? A carpenter? A prophet? A teacher? A revolutionary? A miracle worker? A king? Or God in human form, which He claimed to be? How could anybody be that? Even after Jesus completed His mission and returned to the Father, many people were still scratching their heads.

So when Someone came to take His place—Someone you could not look in the eye or talk with face-to-face—you can understand why the confusion continued. "Is the Spirit Someone we are supposed to get to know?" His followers asked—and are still asking today. If the answer is yes, what a challenge! But what a necessity! Thomas Arnold, eighteenth-century educator, said, "He who does not know God the Holy Spirit cannot know God at all."[2]

That is a provocative statement, but its converse is exciting. For those who do know the Holy Spirit know God. When we talk about going deeper into the Spirit, we are not talking about delving into something apart from God or even tangential to God. We are talking about delving into God Himself—into His very heart.

Can we know Someone we don't understand? Certainly we can. We know our family members, don't we? Do we always understand them? (Don't answer out loud!) Understanding is not a prerequisite to knowing. It may be the other way around. In referring to the Spirit, Samuel Shoemaker says, "We must know Him before we can even try to define Him."[3] So familiarity seems to be a top priority.

Okay, but how do we get to know this most mysterious member of the Godhead? Do we have to be theologians? Absolutely not, responds Dr. R. C. Sproul. "Not every Christian needs to be a seminary-trained theological scholar, but every Christian does need to understand the nature of the God we worship."[4]

SO LET'S BEGIN

Let's find out what the Spirit is like. We'll start with what is considered "the dry stuff." We remember being taught that the Holy Spirit is the third Person of the Trinity, but what does that mean?

According to Professor L. Berkhof in his book about systematic theology, "But in God there are no three individuals alongside of, and separate from one another, but only personal self distinctions within the Divine essence."[5] The operative word in this statement is "personal"—that which pertains to a Person. Indeed, when we are talking about the Spirit, we are not talking about a thing but, rather, about Someone who possesses an intellect, emotions and a will. We are talking about Someone to be referred to as a "He," not an "It." Jesus calls Him our "Helper."

Although the Spirit never changes, different people see different aspects of His nature. Therefore, each individual is inclined to describe Him in a different way. Imagine you are sitting in a room alone. You are waiting to meet the Holy Spirit. First, however, you are to hear testimonies from people who knew Him, believers from both the Old and New Testaments, and from one contemporary Christian. By the time all these people are finished speaking, you hope your understanding of who the Spirit is will be more complete. Those who lived before Messiah came will speak first. Because they do not yet know the Spirit of Christ, they see the third Person of the Trinity as simply

THE SPIRIT OF GOD.

Hearing from the Old Testament Saints

Picture Adam, the first man, stepping into the room. He stops and faces you. "It was God's Spirit," he says, "who breathed into my nostrils the breath of life and I became a living being. So I know Him as the Life Giver." *Wow!*

Now watch Noah, the builder of the ark, enter. "The Spirit of God is Someone to fear," he tells you, "Someone whose voice should be heeded." *Indeed.*

Job, who met God in a storm, takes his place beside the other two. "The Spirit controls nature," he declares. "He draws up the drops of water, which distill as rain to the streams." *An appropriate description for our study*, you think.

Next you hear from Moses, who investigated a burning bush and met the Spirit there. "I know Him as One majestic in holiness, awesome in glory, working wonders," he testifies. *Will He be my miracle worker, too?*

It is Bezalel's turn. You recall he was involved in the construction of the Tent of Meeting. He says, "When I went to fashion the Ark of the Covenant, I felt a supernatural power take over. So to me the Spirit of

God is the Master Craftsman." *Will He bestow upon me any supernatural abilities?* you wonder.

The next speaker is Eldad, one of Moses' elders. "I know the Spirit as Someone who gave me words to say," he declares. *I certainly need that assist,* you concur. These six men are finished, so they nod to you and file out of the room.

The Major Prophets Speak

Enter some of God's prophets, who will now present their views. Elijah, one of God's most respected spokesmen, goes first. "I know the Spirit as One who speaks in a 'gentle whisper,'" he says, "and tells you that you are not alone." *I need that kind of reassurance,* you think.

Elisha, his successor, follows. "When I asked for a double portion of the Spirit who empowered my mentor, my request was honored," he shares. "So I know God's Spirit as One who does above and beyond what is required." *How wonderful!*

Isaiah speaks next. "I know God's Spirit as an Encourager," he testifies. "He will lift you up on eagles' wings and you will soar." *Oh, to have this boost in my downtimes!*

Ezekiel steps forward. While standing by a river in the land of Babylon, he had a vision of some very strange creatures and huge spinning wheels—all of which were obeying God's Spirit. So he says simply, "The Holy Spirit is the Director of some very awesome happenings." *One of these "happenings" is the subject of this book!* you realize.

Daniel, who was known to those in his pagan country as one having "the spirit of the holy gods," had a vision too. "The Spirit resides in the Ancient of Days," he states. Then he adds, "I saw Him flow like a river of fire from the Ancient One who sat on a throne." *Spectacular!* you conclude. After this description, the major prophets leave the room.

The Minor Prophets Testify

The minor prophets enter the room as a unit, taking their places beside each other. You lean forward.

Hosea: "To me the Spirit is a Refresher. He comes down like the winter rains, like the spring rains that water the earth." *Another appropriate description for this study,* you think.

Joel: "To me He is a Promise. He will be poured out in the last days upon your sons and daughters and they will perform wonders." *I can't wait!* you muse.

Amos: "To me He is the Lord Almighty. He touches the earth and it melts. He calls for the waters of the sea and pours them out over the face of the land. The Lord is His name." *Incredible!*

Micah: "To me the Spirit is Power. The mountains melt beneath Him and the valleys split apart, like wax before fire, like water rushing down a slope." *Rush toward me, Lord,* you plead.

Nahum: "To me the Spirit is wind. He has His way in the storm." *Have your way with me, Holy Spirit,* you find yourself praying.

Habakkuk: "To me the Spirit is Radiance. His glory covers the heaven. His splendor is like the sunrise." *Oh, to catch Habakkuk's vision!*

Zephaniah: "You will find the Spirit an intimate Friend. He will take great delight in you; He will quiet you with His love; He will rejoice over you with singing." *How personal!*

Haggai: "The Spirit is One who will remain among you. So do not fear. Ever."[6] *Be my Comforter, please,* you whisper. After this last statement, the Old Testament believers file out of the room.

A Voice from the Twentieth Century

Before the New Testament speakers are called, a twentieth-century Christian enters. He asks to set the stage for those of us privileged to live on this side of the Cross, those of us who view the Holy Spirit as

THE SPIRIT OF CHRIST.

He is the German Pastor Dietrich Bonhoeffer, who was martyred for his faith during World War II. "The Holy Spirit is Christ Himself dwelling in the hearts of the faithful,"[7] he says.

Voices from the New Testament

You look up. A group is entering. Each individual will speak briefly.

To Mary, the mother of Jesus, the Spirit is the One who "overshadowed" her when the miraculous conception took place.

To John the Baptist, He is the One who filled him from birth and enabled him to be another "Elijah," preparing the way of the Lord.

To John the apostle, He is the One who "anoints" believers, enabling them to distinguish truth from error.

To the apostle Peter, He is the One who "rests upon" those who suffer for their faith.

To Ananias and Sapphira, He is Someone you never lie to; for if you do, the consequences could be deadly.

To Stephen, He is One who enables you to endure the pain of death, even death for your faith.

To Simon the Sorcerer, the Spirit is One whose power he coveted so much that he was willing to pay for it. He regretfully acknowledges his error.

To Philip, the Spirit is One who transports people to where a ready witness is waiting and then empowers them to testify.

To the apostle Paul, He is the One who baptizes all believers (Jews and Greek, slave and free, male and female) into one Body and urges them to keep unity.[8]

When these New Testament presenters are finished, they quietly leave. Who is coming in next?

A SURPRISE!

Jesus Speaks

It is Jesus. *Is He going to introduce His own Spirit?* you wonder. *Why, that must be like introducing Himself.* You listen intently.

"I want to acquaint you with the Spirit of the Sovereign Lord," Jesus begins, "The One who is upon Me, the One who has anointed Me to preach the good news to the poor, to bind up the brokenhearted, to proclaim freedom for the captives and release from darkness for the prisoners. He is the Spirit of Truth. He goes out from the Father. He testifies about Me. And He brings glory to Me.

"He descended upon Me at My water baptism in the form of a dove. But He will baptize you with fire. He led Me to the place of temptation and then enabled Me to stand firm against the onslaughts of Satan. He will do the same for you.

"When I told my disciples I would send 'another Helper,'" Jesus continues, "I was referring to Someone like Myself, yet different. Whereas I was the first Helper, He is the second. I dwelt among My people; He dwells within them. I was a temporary resident of Earth; He is a more permanent One. I came in physical form; He, spiritual. Those who receive Me receive My Spirit, who then becomes 'a spring of water welling up to eternal life.' So it behooves all believers everywhere to get to know Him better."[9] After speaking these words, Jesus smiles and leaves the room. You wait.

ENTER THE SPIRIT

The Voice of the Spirit

Suddenly He is there. Right beside you. You see no one. You hear nothing. But you know. You sense His Presence and you feel His love. Should you rise in respect or fall on your face in submission? You do neither. You can't. His holiness has descended upon you so powerfully you are temporarily paralyzed.

"Believer," He begins, "You are mine."

This is amazing, you think. *My ears are hearing no audible sound. But my heart is registering every word.*

"You have been special to Me from the beginning. Before I formed you in the womb, I knew you. I knit you together in your mother's body. When the moment was right for you to emerge into the world, I breathed into your nostrils the breath of life and you became a living soul.

"Just as I gave life to your body, so I also gave life to your spirit. I arranged for your adoption into the family of God. It was I who enabled you to cry 'Abba, Father!' And when you did, I took up residence in your life and made your body My temple. As you know, I immediately began making changes. I started producing through you the fruit of Christlikeness so that everybody you meet would know to Whom you belong.

"I freed you from the bondage of having to keep the law. I credited Christ's righteousness to your account; and on every page of your life where debits were noted, I wrote, 'Paid in full.' I also marked you with a seal, guaranteeing your inheritance as a child of the King. I am here today to promise that I who began this good work in you will carry it to completion. Never will I leave you; never will I forsake you. When the day of resurrection comes, I will be at your grave to give life to your mortal body. I will raise it in power.

"But I promise to be with you now as well, in the nitty-gritty of your daily life. When you don't know where to turn, call on Me and I will counsel you. When you're going through a hard time, I'll be there to comfort you. When you're feeling down, I will lift you up. When you are too weak even to reach out, I will be your strength.

"Should your devotional life ever get stale, I'll show you a new approach. I'll enable you to see things in My Word that are fresh and wonderful. When you have a hard time remembering what I have taught you, I will bring it to your remembrance.

"There will be times when you will be asked to testify to your faith in a public arena and you may be nervous. I want you to know I will be there with you, supplying the words.

"There will also be times when you will be called upon to pray and won't know what to say or how to say it. I will be there then, too, and will intercede for you. You are 'fail safe' in My love. Always remember that.

"I have to warn you, though, that when you sin, I will make you feel guilty. That's because I care. When you repent of your sin, it is Jesus Christ who will forgive you. But I am the One who will hold you close and reassure you that you are God's. Then I will put you back on the road to victory and walk beside you all the way.

"When dangers lie ahead, I will inform you. When you're running close to empty, I will offer to fill you. Little by little I'll transform you into the person the Father wants you to be. I will energize, revitalize, refresh, restore and preserve you. When it's time for you to enter into glory, I'll personally present you to the Father and the Son. I am your Helper, commissioned to work in all things so that in the end you are conformed to the likeness of Jesus Christ.[10]

"That's what you want, isn't it—to be like Jesus? So tell Me, My friend, why are you hesitating to enter into a deeper relationship with Me? Do you need inspiration from some ordinary people who were caught in cloudbursts of blessing?"

Notes
1. John 3:8.
2. Quoted by R. C. Sproul, *The Mystery of the Holy Spirit* (Wheaton, Ill.: Tyndale House Publishers, 1990), p. 10.
3. Samuel M. Shoemaker, *With the Holy Spirit and With Fire* (New York: HarperCollins, 1960), p. 45.
4. Sproul, *The Mystery of the Holy Spirit*, p. 73.
5. L. Berkhof, *Systematic Theology* (Grand Rapids: Wm. B. Eerdmans Publishing Co., 1939), p. 87.
6. Old Testament speakers' remarks are based on the following Scripture references: Genesis 2:7; 6:7; Job 36:27; Exodus 15:11; 31:1-3; Numbers 11:25-30; 1 Kings 19:9-18;

2 Kings 2:1-18; Isaiah 40:31; Ezekiel 1:26,27; 2:4; Daniel 4:8; 7:9,10; Hosea 6:3; Joel 2:28-30; Amos 9:5,6; Micah 1:4; Nahum 1:3; Habakkuk 3:3,4; Zephaniah 3:17; Haggai 2:5.

7. Dietrich Bonhoeffer, *The Cost of Discipleship* (Indianapolis: The Macmillan Company, 1963), p. 259.

8. New Testament speakers' remarks are based on the following Scripture references: Luke 1:35; 1:15-17; 1 John 2:27; 1 Peter 4:12-14; Acts 5:1-11; 7:54-60; 8:18-25; 8:26-40; 1 Corinthians 12:13; Ephesians 4:3.

9. Jesus' remarks are based on the following Scripture verses: Isaiah 61:1-3; John 15:26; 16:14; Matthew 3:16; 3:11; 4:1-11.

10. The Spirit's remarks are based on the following Scripture references: Jeremiah 1:5; Psalm 139:13; Genesis 2:7; John 3:6; Romans 8:16; 1 Corinthians 6:19; Romans 8:15; Galatians 5:22,23; Romans 8:2; 4:24; Ephesians 1:13; Philippians 1:6; Hebrews 13:5; Romans 8:11,14; 2 Corinthians 1:4; Psalm 10:17; 2 Corinthians 12:9; John 16:13; 1 Corinthians 2:12; John 14:26; Mark 13:11; Romans 8:26; John 16:8; 1 John 2:12; 5:13; Acts 20:23; Ephesians 5:18; 2 Corinthians 3:18; Psalm 119:93 (compilation of several versions and paraphrases); 2 Corinthians 5:4,5; Romans 8:28,29.

Cloudbursts of Blessing

"I will pour water on the thirsty land,
and streams on the dry ground."

ISAIAH 44:3

Three years without rain. Three years of dehydrating sun. Three years in which to become desperate for the heavens to open up and pour out a blessing.

This drought has come as a judgment. The Israelites, led by evil King Ahab, have turned their backs on the one true God in favor of the Canaanite god of fertility. So the Lord has withheld rain. Famine results.

Enter this scene, if you will, through your imagination. Listen to God as He is instructing His prophet Elijah. God is saying, "'Go and present yourself to Ahab, and I will send rain on the land.'"[1]

Elijah does. The encounter leads to Mount Carmel, where a confrontation occurs between the prophet of God and the prophets of Baal. It is agreed that both parties will call on their respective gods and whichever god answers by fire, that is the one true God.

Baal's prophets go first. They build their altar and prepare their sacrifice. Then they call on their god to light the fire. Nothing happens. So they start shouting and dancing. Still nothing happens. As a last resort, they slash themselves with swords, letting their blood flow, but the heavens continue to remain silent.

Now it is Elijah's turn. He builds his altar and prepares his sacrifice. He asks the people to drench everything with water, even though it is in short supply. They do. When all is ready, Elijah prays. The answer is instantaneous. Fire descends and burns up the soggy offering. It does more than that, however. It consumes the wood, the stones and the soil as well. Then it travels the trenches surrounding the altar and licks up the water there. Wow! The one true God has spoken.

His people know it. They have sinned and they have paid the price. In addition, they have been reminded afresh of who is in control. Now it is time for God's judgment to be lifted and the windows of heaven to be unlocked. Elijah cups his ears of faith. "I hear a mighty downpour coming," he announces.

"Go and look toward the sea," he commands his servant. The boy does so but comes back disappointed. Not a cloud is in sight.

"Go back," Elijah tells him. Again no clouds. This exchange takes place seven times, we are told. Then it happens: "The sky grew black with clouds, the wind rose, a heavy rain came,"[2] the Bible says.

Imagine the scene: Ahab is driving his chariot full speed down the mountainside. Elijah, empowered in a special way by God's Spirit, is running even faster than Ahab is driving. People everywhere are celebrating this blessing from heaven.

This picture takes me back to those days on the farm when I celebrated relief from the drought that affected our family. It doesn't matter what century you live in, I guess, or even what millennium. Rain makes a difference. Rain lifts spirits.

RAIN RESTORES HOPE

Jesus' disciples learn this in a powerfully spiritual way. As we visit them right after their Master's death, we see a pretty discouraged lot. Following Jesus has consumed them. Now He is gone. So is their hope. They are trying to pick up their lives by going back to their old routines, but it is hard. Their hearts are elsewhere. What does the future hold for this bewildered bunch? Plenty, we know.

On the Day of Pentecost as the disciples are meeting together, the Spirit rains down upon them. This "cloudburst" is accompanied by a violent wind and flames of fire, we are told, yet it has a personal touch to it, too. Andrew Murray sums it up this way: "The Holy Spirit came down to the disciples direct from the heart of their exalted Lord, bringing down unto them the glorious life of heaven into which He had entered."[3] In other words, when Jesus poured out His Spirit on His disciples, He poured out His very own power.

> The Holy Spirit dropped on this parched and thirsty band. Because He did, the world would never be the same.

The change in the disciples is incredible. The depressed are now exuberant. The timid have been made bold. The empty are filled to overflowing. You can read about their new beginnings in the thrilling book of Acts. As Dr. Luke, the author, describes the rapid spread of Christianity from region to region, it is almost impossible not to experience his excitement.

It seems as though you are there as individuals begin hearing the Word of God, each in his or her own language. You are there as thousands commit their lives to Jesus Christ, some after listening to the good news only once. You are there as the lame walk, the blind see, the deaf hear and the demon possessed are set free. You are there as religious and political authorities decide they must do something about this growing menace called Christianity. You are also there as Jesus' followers determine to keep right on preaching the gospel, even if it costs them their lives. The events Dr. Luke describes are so supercharged that Bible translator J. B. Phillips is reported to have said, "The work of translating the book of Acts was very much like wiring a house with the electrical current turned on."

What made the difference in these spiritually dry believers? What revitalized them? Rain, that's what. Rain. The Holy Spirit dropped on this parched and thirsty band. Because He did, the world would never be the same. New life would spring up everywhere. It would multiply and replenish the earth.

Become Peter

Picture yourself getting ready to address this huge crowd that has gathered to witness the strange events of Pentecost. You are nervous. You can't imagine why this job of preaching has fallen to you. After all, you are the disciple who failed the Master when He needed you most. You wish you could stop the mental video of that occasion from playing in your mind, but you can't. In fact, it is playing right now.

Jesus has just been arrested and taken to the high priest's courtyard. You are standing by a charcoal fire near the door. You are warming your hands. One of your group has just betrayed the Master and you were a witness to the scene. It is hard to sort out your feelings.

Suddenly someone approaches and asks, "You are not one of His disciples, are you?" The words startle you.

"I am not," you blurt out in self-defense.

Then you go on to repeat your denial two more times. The smoke from the charcoal fire is twirling past your nostrils, causing your eyes to water. It wasn't that long ago that you had promised to die for your Lord. Now you are finding it hard to live for Him. What a disappointment you are, especially to yourself.

Your mental video goes into fast forward. Past Jesus' trial it whirls, past the sentencing, the crucifixion, the burial, even the empty tomb. It stops on that night after the Resurrection when you are back on the Sea of Tiberias, trying to rejuvenate your fishing career.

As the darkness lifts and the dawn is beginning to lighten the skies, you notice a familiar figure standing on the shore. You leap from your boat and splash toward Him. When you reach the beach, you stop short. That smell! Jesus is cooking breakfast over a charcoal fire. You remember the last time you were near a charcoal fire. It was the time you betrayed your Lord. You wipe the sting from your eyes and look into His eyes.

"Peter, do you love me?" He asks.

You are stunned. This word for love connotes the highest form of commitment—a love that requires personal sacrifice. You want to answer yes, but you are an honest person. You have to tell it like it is.

"I am fond of you," you respond, falling short of the answer Jesus is looking for from you.

Jesus asks the question again; you give the same answer. Then Jesus rephrases His question: "Peter, are you fond of Me?"

"Yes, Lord, you know that I am fond of you," you reply. Then it hits you: three denials, three chances to make it right. And you have failed. Again. Chalk up six zeroes. You might as well give up.

No wonder you are amazed to be Christ's spokesperson to this crowd that has gathered before you right now. Here you are being faced with the necessity of preaching the gospel to thousands of people, and you are convinced you are not the right person for the job.

You think, *Maybe this is another test. But I fail tests. I wish Jesus were here. He never fails anything.*

Then you remember. He *is* here. You can feel His Spirit beginning to stir within you. You know if you submit, Jesus' Spirit will do the task for you. Giving up control, however, is a new discipline for you. You are not sure you can do it, but you would like to try.

Let's see how it goes, you think.

You begin by letting the Spirit collect your scattered thoughts. *Good!* Now you let Him select the right one to express first. *That's it!* You listen intently as the words start coming out. They are articulate and convincing. *Amazing! This isn't me talking,* you think.

Then you hear yourself quoting from the book of Joel. "I will pour out my Spirit on all people," you are saying. "Even on my servants, both men and women, I will pour out my Spirit in those days" (2:28,29).

As you are talking, it hits you. *"Those days" are now. Scripture is being fulfilled as I am quoting it—right now! And it is happening through me!* You feel as if you are being drenched by a heavenly downpour. You continue, "And everyone who calls on the name of the Lord will be saved" (v. 32).[4]

They are. Your eyes open wider and wider as listeners start responding to the gospel invitation. They keep coming and coming to give their lives to Jesus Christ. Three thousand of them at final count. As the "rain" continues to come down, everyone within hearing range gets "wet." They have witnessed supernatural power surging through an unschooled, ordinary man, and they are astonished. So are you.

Become Stephen

You are a man described in the Bible as being "full of faith and of the Holy Spirit." You work miracles in the name of your Lord and, like Peter, find yourself being called before the authorities. As you open your mouth to make your case, you feel a holy boldness come upon you. You submit to it. "You stiff-necked people, with uncircumcised hearts and ears!" you hear yourself saying. "You are just like your fathers: You always resist the Holy Spirit!"

Uh-oh! Your sermon is too much for this ruling body of Hebrews. They are furious. You who are full of the Holy Spirit keep your cool, though. You look up to heaven and catch a vision of the glory of God. It is so inspiring that you feel you can now go through almost anything.

Your worst fears are realized. The angry mob picks up stones, then hurls them at you. As rock after rock pelts your body, you feel your legs beginning to buckle. As you fall, a supernatural compassion rains down upon you, and you cry, "Lord, do not hold this sin against them."

As you drift in and out of consciousness, dying seems like going to sleep in the arms of your Lord. Before you close your eyes for the last time, however, you catch sight of that infamous persecutor of Christians named Saul. He is sanctioning your death. What you don't realize, of course, is that Saul himself will soon be converted to Christianity and eventually join you and other martyrs for their faith. Truly God's ways are mysterious.[5]

Become Saul/Paul

You are a Pharisee trained under the recognized teacher Gamaliel; you are a "Hebrew of the Hebrews," so to speak. Your assignment is to purge your religion of a dangerous sect, and you have been doing so with a zeal few leaders can match.

After Stephen's death, you decide to proceed on to Damascus to take some more religious prisoners. As you are walking along the road, trying to concentrate on the mission before you, you can't get the image of Stephen's countenance out of your mind. Talk about mental videos stuck on "replay." Over and over you keep seeing that face. It is glowing like the face of an angel. *Why, Stephen looks as if he is seeing God!*

Who is this Jesus, you wonder, *who is commanding such loyalty even after His death?*

In a moment you find out. A white hot light streaks from the skies and knocks you to the ground. In the confusion you hear a voice. It is Jesus! While you are trying to get over the shock of listening to the One whose followers you have been persecuting, you struggle to get up. You can't see a thing. You have been blinded, but spiritually your eyes have been opened.

This One you set out to destroy, you now acknowledge as your Savior and your Lord. Strange though it may sound, you want to proclaim His message to the world.

After a period of time, your new assignment begins. "Boldly and without hindrance," the Bible says, you preach the kingdom of God and teach about Jesus Christ. As you go from place to place, you are aware of an internal Guide. It is almost as if He is telling you ahead of time what you will be facing. At one point you declare, "And now, compelled by the Spirit, I am going to Jerusalem, not knowing what will happen to me there. I only know that in every city the Holy Spirit warns me that prison and hardships are facing me."

They come as predicted, but the One who warns you is also faithful to fortify you. You hear yourself saying, "I am ready not only to be bound but also to die in Jerusalem for the name of the Lord Jesus."

As you come to what appears to be the end of your days, you review your life. You have been imprisoned, flogged, stoned and shipwrecked. You have been "in danger from rivers, in danger from bandits, in danger from [your] own countrymen, in danger from Gentiles; in danger in the city, in danger in the country, in danger at sea; and in danger from false brothers." You have gone without food, sleep and clothing. What else can happen to you?

> We Christians at the beginning
> of a new millennium know the
> answers: The gates of hell will
> not overcome Christ's Church.

"I know what it is to be in need, and I know what it is to have plenty," you conclude. "I have learned the secret of being content in any and every situation....I can do everything through him who gives me strength." What a tribute to the Spirit! He has rained down upon you in power, and you can't stop praising Him. You are thankful you got caught in a "thunderstorm" and you are grateful for the "lightning" that changed your life.[6]

As you contemplate the future, you find yourself looking past your own death. How will the Church fare? Will attempts to stifle it only make it stronger? Will other Sauls have their names changed to Paul?

LISTEN TO CONTEMPORARIES

We Christians at the beginning of a new millennium know the answers: The gates of hell will not overcome Christ's Church. Yes, there will be more believers through whom the Spirit moves powerfully. In a book called *They Found the Secret,* V. Raymond Edman features recent Christians who, like the disciples, were caught in cloudbursts of blessing. Edman notes, however, that none of them was empowered from on high without first coming to the end of him or herself. Summing up the difference "rain" makes, Edman says, "The pattern seems to be: self-centeredness, self effort, increasing dissatisfaction and other discouragements, a temptation to give it all up because there is no better way; and then finding the Spirit of God to be their strength, their guide, their confidence and companion—in a word, their life."[7]

Charles Swindoll, a contemporary author, agrees. "Without Christ you and I were like a vast empty reservoir awaiting the coming of a downpour. As salvation became a reality, this emptiness became full to the point of running over. The Spirit of God has filled our internal capacity with power and dynamic."[8]

MAKE IT PERSONAL

So what about you? Now that you are back inside your own skin, do you, like those before you, long to be drenched with refreshment from on high? If you are dry enough, you do. For only those who are thirsty long for water. Only those who know they are parched appreciate a downpour.

"As the deer pants for streams of water," the psalmist says, "so my soul pants for you, O God."[9] It is a plea from a thirsty heart.

There is a big difference, though, between a drink and a downpour. You may feel you are ready for the former, but you are not sure you are ready for the latter. That is okay. Maybe your fear is legitimate. Perhaps even necessary. Let's see.

Notes

1. First Kings 18:1.
2. First Kings 18:45.
3. Andrew Murray, *Abide in Christ* (Fort Washington, Pa.: Christian Literature Crusade, 1968), p. 157.
4. Peter's account is based on the following Scripture verses: John 18:17; 21:15-17; Acts 2:17,18,21.
5. Stephen's account is based on the following Scripture references: Acts 6:5; 7:51,60.

6. Saul/Paul's account is based on the following Scripture verses: Acts 28:31; 20:23; 21:13; 2 Corinthians 11:26; Philippians 4:12,13.

7. V. Raymond Edman, *They Found the Secret* (Grand Rapids: Zondervan Publishing House, 1960), Introduction.

8. Charles Swindoll, *Living Closer to the Flame* (Dallas, Tex.: Word Publishing, 1993), p. 116.

9. Psalm 42:1.

4

A Reason to Fear

~~~~~~~~~~

"If he holds back the waters, there is drought;
if he lets them loose, they devastate the land."

JOB 12:15

DANGER! DO NOT GO BEYOND THIS POINT. THE WAVES HERE ARE STRONG AND UNPREDICTABLE. SEVERAL PERSONS HAVE BEEN SWEPT FROM THESE ROCKS INTO THE SEA.

WARNING! CHECK THE CHART TO YOUR RIGHT FOR THE TIME OF THE NEXT HIGH TIDE. THIS AREA FLOODS IN SECONDS. DON'T BE CAUGHT UNAWARES.

CAUTION! THIS ROAD IS DANGEROUS DURING STORMS. IF THE YELLOW LIGHT IS FLASHING, PROCEED SLOWLY. WAVES BREAK OVER THE SEAWALL WITHOUT WARNING.

So read some of the signs and placards encountered when traveling. All of them alert us to the hazards of water. All give us reason to fear.

Our fears go beyond signs, however. Courtesy of the six o'clock news, we can see with our own eyes the devastation water sometimes causes. In fact, we view the destruction while it is taking place. We watch, in horror, as houses are shoved off their foundations and swept downstream in pieces. We witness boats being torn from their moorings and deposited in people's front yards. We stare at flood victims clinging to trees as a river of passing debris rushes by below. We watch heroic attempts at rescue; some succeed and some fail. Although we experience these scenes vicariously, they are as real as if we were physically present. Well, almost.

I invite you to come to our apartment. You are now on the fourteenth floor of a high-rise at the edge of the Atlantic Ocean. The storm of '92 is about to hit. You drag a chair to a window. You don't want to miss a thing!

The rain is gentle at first. Then as the wind rises, water starts coming down in torrents. At times it looks and sounds as if God is slapping sheets against your windows. You glance over at the chandelier and notice it is swinging.

What's that noise in the kitchen? You decide to investigate. It is water gurgling in the pipes.

You go down the hall to see what is happening in the bathroom. As you open the door, your eyes are drawn to the toilet bowl. Waves are splashing in their own little ocean. This storm is bigger than you thought it would be. You send up a prayer for divine protection.

You return to your perch in the living room. The plate glass windows are vibrating. *These panes are guaranteed to withstand gusts over a hundred miles an hour,* you reassure yourself.

I just wish I could remember how much over!

How powerful is this gale anyway? Thanks to your husband's craftsmanship, you can find out. You check the digital readout that is connected to an outside wind gauge. It is registering zero. *How can that be?* You strain to see through the pelting rain: *where is the gauge?* You spot only its holder; the rest has been blown to pieces. You shoot off another prayer.

As you look down at the parking deck adjacent to your building, you notice that waves are breaking over the east wall, showering the neat rows of cars with salt water. Suddenly a surge of sea pours onto the concrete, spinning cars around and slamming them into each other. You cannot believe your eyes.

You race down the stairs (the elevators are out of operation) to the underground garage to check on your own car, which you thought was parked in relative safety. As you approach the door to the garage, you see a sign: "No access." The garage is flooded with seawater. Every car has been "totaled." Your heart sinks.

The person at the front desk gives you more news. The high-rise next door has given up its fight against the elements. The managers have decided to open the doors facing the ocean, as well as the door facing the street, to let the ocean run through. You hear it is doing just that.

You grope your way back up 14 flights of stairs, which, since the power is off, are now in total darkness. You don't know what else to do, so you reclaim your seat by the windows, which are still vibrating but intact. The roar outside is thunderous. You thank God for His protection, but you can't help pulling your chair back a little.

> Water can be both destructive
> and beneficial. It is a strange
> dichotomy.

As you strain to make out what is what on the ground below, you gasp. Water is everywhere, as far as the eye can see. Your town has been inundated. You can't distinguish any property lines, front lawns, backyards or streets. Only buildings. Houses, garages, a church, a store and a school are sticking up here and there out of the sea.

A military amphibian is coming down what used to be Ocean Avenue, rescuing the elderly, the ill and the fearful. You watch as it maneuvers around logs, planks, tables, lawn chairs, life-guard paraphernalia, roofing materials, concrete dividers, boats and a host of other reminders of the way life used to be, of the order that existed before the water came.

After three days of pounding, the storm abates. Electrical power is eventually restored, and your car, along with many others, is towed out of the muddy garage. You are thankful for the Lord's protection, both of yourself and of your apartment, which have remained dry. You let Him know. As you pray, however, you realize the storm has accomplished something positive. You have a new appreciation for the power of water, a new appreciation for the power of God.

As you look down upon your town, you remember that some of these houses, now flooded, were in need of repair even before the storm. They will get it, more quickly in fact than if there had been no natural disaster.

No home owner would choose tragedy as a means of bringing about improvements, but it does the job. So it is in the spiritual realm. Floods speed up the process of sanctification. It is amazing how God works.

The water He sends can be both destructive and beneficial. The seas that flooded your town are the same seas you frolicked in last summer. The waters of the Niagara River that take the lives of those who get too close to the falls provide you and millions of others with electricity to light your homes, cook your meals and wash your clothes. It is a strange dichotomy.

Become Noah

There is sin in the land. Along with sin comes God's warning: "My Spirit will not contend with man forever,....I am going to bring floodwaters on the earth to destroy all life under the heavens."[1]

What does the Lord mean by "floodwaters"? Until now you have watched gentle mists sustain the earth. The thought of a flood sounds scary, but who are you to question almighty God? So you build the ark He commands, and you do so according to His specifications.

At the appointed time the rain begins. For 40 days it will continue. The people that mocked you as you were preparing your shelter are now becoming concerned. They want in. God's instructions were explicit, though: Only representatives of each animal and bird and the eight members of your family are to enter the ark.

You watch from inside as the waters rise and people scramble to higher ground. Suddenly a fountain underneath you erupts and your boat shoots skyward. Several stragglers have been lifted by the upsurge. You hear them pounding on the planks. You also hear voices. Some are low and gruff. Others are high pitched and frantic. You even recognize the thin, fragile voices of children. The voices cry, plead, curse, bargain and scream. Together they compose a haunting symphony. You realize God would normally expect you to reach out to the hurting, the dying and other victims of natural disasters. In this case, however, to do so would be to disobey Him. Keeping the door of that ark closed is the hardest thing you will ever have to do. You do it though. You must.

At last there is silence—awful, lonely silence. The only thing you can hear now is the creaking of the ark as it rocks up and down on the rising sea. You breathe a sigh of relief. Finally, it is over.

Become Job

Like Noah, you have just been through a terrible storm. Messengers come to you bearing news. It is not good. A mighty wind has destroyed the house in which your children were having a party and all 10 of them have died. Lightning has struck your sheep and killed the servants that were shepherding them. Looters have raided your oxen and camels and carried them away. As if this isn't enough pain to cope with, you come down with a disease that hurts, itches and is disfiguring.

You turn to your wife for comfort, but she is struggling with her own loss. After all, the children were hers too. She mothered them. So instead of offering you the embrace you need, she lashes out in frustration, blaming you for these calamities.

Your friends try to help, but they too think that a series of tragedies as awful as these must be the result of someone's sin. You are suspect. Remembering what happened to the "sinners" in Noah's day, you can understand your friends' conclusion. Their remarks still hurt though. Although you recognize that tragedy can be a judgment of God, it isn't always. In fact, most of the time it is not. After all, we live in a fallen world and trouble befalls everybody. As far as you are concerned, you see no connection at all between anything you have done and what has happened to your family, to your fortune and to your health.

One day as you are sitting in the sand, listening to your friends philosophize, the skies begin to darken. You are so engrossed in their arguments, however, you hardly notice the change. Then the thunder rolls. You are startled. Lightning streaks across the sky. You gaze up. A droplet of moisture falls on your skin. Then another and another. It is starting to rain. You are about to be the victim of another storm, and you are afraid.

Everyone runs for cover. You can't run. Your physical condition, like everything else, is part of God's providence. Here you are, all alone in the storm, but not for long. The God you have been questioning begins to speak. As you listen, you expect Him to give you some answers. He doesn't. Instead, He asks some questions of His own.

"Were you there when I created the earth? Can you explain My sovereignty? Can you duplicate My power? Can you diagram My workings?" These queries comprise the essence of the Lord's questions, but they are posed in many different ways. At one point the barrage becomes embarrassing. "If you want to take My place and chart your own life, 'then adorn yourself with glory and splendor, and clothe yourself in honor and majesty,'"[2] the Lord says. In other words, "If you want to play Me, you should look like Me."

You are humbled. You cannot reply. You realize you are seeing God as He really is for the very first time. It has all happened through a storm.

> The vehicle God used to strip you He is now using to draw you closer to His heart. There is nothing to do but to worship.

The vehicle God used to strip you He is now using to draw you closer to His heart. There is nothing to do but to worship.

Become Moses

You are leading God's people out of Egypt. Thousands of men, women and children, and carts full of belongings and animals that don't necessarily want to go, are struggling along at your command. You come to the Red Sea.

Now what? Pharaoh's army is in hot pursuit behind you and a threatening body of water stretches before you. God has taken care of you in the past, and you are confident He will care for you now, but how?

As you raise your staff over the water, a miracle happens. "The waters were divided, and the Israelites went through the sea on dry ground, with a wall of water on their right and on their left,"[3] the Bible says.

What an experience this is, you think, as you watch this horde of people proceeding between the mounds of water stacked on either side. Some are walking; others are running. A few are glancing right, then left, but most are focusing on the distant shore. A young man at the end of the line provides some comic relief. As he runs, he is holding out his hands, palms toward the "walls" as if to say, "Just one more minute, Lord. Don't forget me!"

At last the long parade of humanity is safe on the other side. You stretch out your staff again, and a reverse miracle occurs. The walls of water meet. Slam! Their joining is so powerful the entire army of Pharaoh is drowned. Later you will record, "Not one of them survived."[4]

Become Jonah

God has just told you to go to Nineveh to preach against the sin in that city, but you don't want to do it. So you board a ship going in the opposite direction. You don't get very far before a violent storm arises, causing concern to all on board. Who is responsible for this calamity?

You know who. You feel guilty, really guilty. You are going to have to confess your disobedience. After all, it is one thing to die for your own sin, but another to take a whole boatload of people with you.

"Pick me up and throw me into the sea," you propose. "It is my fault that this great storm has come upon you."[5]

The sailors protest; but as the storm is getting wilder, they feel they have no other option. Over the side you go. The sea grows calm.

Those on board recognize the workings of the one true God and acknowledge that He controls people's destinies. They make sacrifices and take vows, we are told.

They are not the only ones communicating with the Lord, however. As you thrash around in the deep, you pray. Then you submit to the elements. You wonder what it feels like to drown. You don't have long to think about it. Suddenly you feel yourself being swept into a huge cavern and propelled down a strange, mushy tunnel. *It's pulsating! It's alive! I've been swallowed by something that's alive!*

While you are trying to figure out whether it is better to die by drowning or by suffocation inside the putrid belly of a sea creature, you realize you are not dead. *It stinks in here,* you think, *but I'm still breathing! God has miraculously provided, and I want to thank Him:*

> You hurled me into the deep, into the very heart of the seas, and the currents swirled about me; all your waves and breakers swept over me. The engulfing waters threatened me, the deep surrounded me; seaweed was wrapped around my head. To the roots of the mountains I sank down; the earth beneath barred me in forever. But you brought my life up from the pit, O Lord my God.[6]

Indeed God did, and He is about to effect an even greater deliverance. Get ready. This huge fish, which has served as your protector, starts retching. It heaves and heaves, trying to rid itself of this thing that is caught in its throat. You are thrown back and forth. Then in one final convulsion you are propelled into fresh air. You feel yourself falling and guess you are going to drown after all. Instead, you land with a thump upon dry ground.

> God has given His rebellious child a second chance! I guess I'd better shape up.

A second chance, you say to yourself. *God has given His rebellious child a second chance! I guess I'd better shape up.*

Become a Disciple in a Boat

At the instruction of your Master you are out on a lake. He has told you He will meet you on the other side. As you are rowing, evening falls. With it the winds pick up; so do the waves. You are being tossed about like a cork.

Suddenly you look up and see Jesus. He is walking on the water, and He isn't sinking! It must be His ghost! You are afraid. Then Jesus speaks. Matthew records this exchange:

> "Take courage! It is I. Don't be afraid."
>
> "Lord, if it's you," Peter replied, "tell me to come to you on the water."
>
> "Come," he said.
>
> Then Peter got down out of the boat, walked on the water and came toward Jesus. But when he saw the wind, he was afraid and, beginning to sink, cried out, "Lord, save me!"
>
> Immediately Jesus reached out his hand and caught him. "You of little faith," he said, "why did you doubt?"
>
> And when they climbed into the boat, the wind died down. Then those who were in the boat worshiped him, saying, "Truly you are the Son of God."[7]

SOME OBSERVATIONS

Because of its ability to destroy, water is something to fear. "If the Lord had not been on our side—" the psalmist says, speaking symbolically, "the flood would have engulfed us, the torrent would have swept over us, the raging waters would have swept us away."[8] The Lord was on David's side, however, as He is on the side of all His children, and that makes all the difference.

When floodwaters come, they remind us who is in control. We realize how powerless we are. We turn to God. Once we see Him in all His awesome majesty and reach out to Him for help, He reaches back in tenderness and takes our hands. It is then that He invites us to step into the flow. "See, I am doing a new thing!" God announces to the prophet Isaiah. "Now it springs up; do you not perceive it? I am making a way in the desert and streams in the wasteland...to give drink to my people, my chosen, the people I formed for myself that they may proclaim my praise."[9]

So we face a decision: when to fear and when to trust. Can we fear *and* trust, both at the same time? Should we?

Oswald Chambers is reported to have said, "The remarkable thing about fearing God is that when you fear God, you fear nothing else, whereas if you do not fear God, you fear everything else."

But how does this combination of fear and trust affect me and my personal worship? Will I be able to say with the hymn writer, "'Twas grace that taught my heart to fear, and grace my fears relieved"[10]—all in the same breath?

Let's find out.

Notes

1. Genesis 6:3,17.
2. Job 40:10.
3. Exodus 14:21,22.
4. Exodus 14:28.
5. Jonah 1:12.
6. Jonah 2:3,5,6.
7. Matthew 14:27-33.
8. Psalm 124:1,4,5.
9. Isaiah 43:19-21.
10. John Newton, "Amazing Grace," verse 2.

5

A Holy Boldness

Let us then approach the throne of grace with
confidence, so that we may receive mercy and find
grace to help us in our time of need.

HEBREWS 4:16

Become Queen Esther

Imagine you are Queen Esther, Hebrew wife of King Xerxes of Persia.
Until now you have been successful in hiding your sensitive nationality.
You are not sure, however, how long you can continue to do so.

One day you learn the palace has issued an edict: "Destroy, kill and
annihilate all the Jews—young and old, women and little children—on a
single day." That day is coming soon—too soon.

What can be done? You love your people dearly and desperately want
them to be spared; but who has influence?

"You," declares your cousin Mordecai. "You must approach the king
and plead on behalf of our people."

Me? you think. *Why, that would require me to reveal my background.
Then I would be killed with the rest of the Jews. I'll probably be killed
anyway because whoever approaches the king without a summons is
subject to the death penalty. The only exception is for the king to extend
the gold scepter and spare the life of the intruder.*

Mordecai understands the risk. Yet he is persistent in urging you to take it. After all, you are someone who has access to the king. It is you or nobody. "And who knows," he asks, "but that you have come to royal position for such a time as this?"

That does it! You commit. You do, however, ask your people to fast and pray as you prepare for your perilous confrontation. "Then," you assure them, "I will go to the king, even though it is against the law. And if I perish, I perish."

So, spiritually fortified yet trembling, you dress in your royal robe and stand in the inner court of the palace. The king is on his throne, scepter in his hand. You wait.

Suddenly he sees you. Your legs turn to water and your heart leaps into your throat. *What will he do?* You remain motionless, your eyes on the scepter.

It is beginning to move. The crowned ball is being thrust toward me. Whew! I'm safe. You have no time now to dwell on personal matters. You have a mission to fulfill. So you approach the king and invite him to a banquet (you don't want to share your real request right away).

Your strategy proves successful. In the end (it is a complicated story), the king revokes his murderous edict and your people are spared. As for you, you are grateful—grateful you were endowed with boldness to approach the king, yet equally grateful you were given wisdom to do so with the respect his position warranted.[1]

Become Moses (Again)

God has instructed you to meet with Him on Mount Sinai. His presence will come down in fire. The people will be allowed to watch the spectacle from below, but on penalty of death they are not to set foot upon the mountain. The time for your encounter will be signaled by a trumpet blast.

You wait. You listen. You watch the mountain. On the third day a cloud descends on the peak. Your heart skips a beat. God is preparing the meeting place.

Suddenly veins of lightning streak from the cloud, and thunder bellows from within it. You listen in awe as a rumble rolls down the mountainside. The ground beneath you begins to shake. The people beside you start trembling. Then you hear it: the sound of the ram's horn. *I must go to the top. Now.*

You step out from the crowd and enter the area that is restricted. *Uh-oh! The ground beneath my feet is shifting. Will it swallow me?* you wonder. *Maybe I should turn back, but the ram's horn is calling me upward. I must advance.*

The closer you get to the top, the darker it gets. The night is so thick you can't see a thing. You have no choice but to stop. Then it descends: the promised fire from on high. You are familiar with fire. God spoke to you from a burning bush. From what you can remember, that fire didn't smoke. This fire's smoke is billowing. It is engulfing you. You squint, you cough and you shield your face, which feels as though it is burning up.

You are about to throw yourself to the ground when Someone shoves you into the cleft of a nearby rock. You open your eyes in time to see the afterglow of God's glory passing by. It is awesome. You bow your head and wait.

The Lord speaks. He wants to give you a set of rules, He says, by which your people are to live. You listen carefully, mentally recording every word. Later, 10 of these commandments will be written on stone, but now you think you have to remember them.

> [God] who initiated this meeting gave you wisdom how to approach Him...with a certain boldness, yet with great reverence.

By the time you leave the mountain, you have experienced the presence of God's Spirit in such a powerful way that your face is literally aglow with His glory. How can you describe the encounter? You are not sure. On the one hand, you have seen God as a "consuming fire," yet on the other, He has expressed His personal interest in you by hiding you in the cleft of a rock. One thing you are sure of: You are grateful that the One who initiated this meeting gave you wisdom as to how to approach Him. The proper way was with a certain boldness, yet with great reverence.[2]

Become Aaron
You are now Moses' brother. You, too, have had your time with God on Mount Sinai. Just recently, though, you were selected to become a high priest. You do not take your responsibilities lightly. As part of your ordi-

nation ceremony, you were bathed from head to toe in a symbolic puri-
fying ritual. As the water touched various parts of your body, you dedicated those parts, one by one, to God.

Then you were anointed with oil. As you felt the smooth liquid cours-
ing down your forehead, eyelids, ears, lips, arms and legs, you prayed that
what you would be thinking about, looking at, listening to, saying, doing
and following would be pleasing to your sovereign Lord.

Next, you recall, a ram was killed. You always did have trouble watching life spill out of a living creature, and this time was no exception.
Some of its blood was collected and dabbed on you: on your right ear,
thumb and big toe. As you felt the touch of the liquid, which this time
was warm, you were reminded afresh that for sin to be forgiven in you
or in anyone else, blood had to be spilled. Then what you heard, what
you did and where you decided to go could be consecrated to a God who
demands holiness.

You are thinking about this ceremony now, on this, the Day of
Atonement, as you stand in the Tabernacle facing the drapery that sepa-
rates the holy of holies from the holy place. As high priest, you are
required to enter the restricted area and "make a covering" for the sins
of your people. It is an awesome task, so, naturally, you are nervous.

You have been warned to perform your duties according to rigid
specifications. If you don't, you could be struck dead. You look at the
rope that has been tied to your ankle, and shake the bells that have
been sewn to your robe. If the people hear the bells, they will know
you are okay. If too long a time passes without any sound, they will
assume you are dead and make plans to drag your body from the area
where only the high priest is allowed to go. You sigh just thinking about
all this.

As you stand there, the drapery looming before you, you replay your
instructions: *Slip behind the curtain and face the Shekinah, that burst
of glory that indicates the presence of God's Holy Spirit. Generate
smoke by placing incense upon the burning coals in the censer. Trust
that it envelops the glory. Sprinkle the mercy seat with blood from an
animal that has just been killed. Then leave. Quickly. There is no room
for error.*

You are ready. Yet as you draw back the curtain and catch a glimpse of
the blinding glow behind it, you feel your chest beginning to tighten.
Nevertheless, you do enter. You have to, but you can't help showing great
respect for the One you are approaching.[3]

Become Isaiah

King Uzziah of Judah has just died. You were comfortable under his reign. Now you have no place to turn except to God.

One day, through a vision, you are ushered into a temple. It is there that you see Him: the sovereign Lord in all His majestic splendor. In your vision He is dressed in a royal robe and seated on a very high throne. You know a monarch's importance is reflected in the length of His train, so you find yourself doing a mental calculation of the extension of His long cloak. It just keeps going and going. Why, it fills the entire temple! You have never met a King like this One!

Two angels, you notice, are hovering above the throne. They are extolling the virtues of the King. "Holy, holy, holy" they chant, "is the Lord Almighty."

> When the voice of the Lord booms from the throne, asking for someone to be His spokesman, you are quick to answer, "Here am I, Lord. Send me!"

As you listen, their words seem to bounce off the support poles of the temple. You look up. The beams are beginning to vibrate. Suddenly the whole structure starts to wobble. *Is it going to collapse and trap me inside? Now the place is filling with smoke!* As you rub the sting from your eyes, you are conscious you are in the presence of a holy God. His Spirit is invading the room. You are terrified—and overcome by a sense of your own unworthiness. *What am I doing here?* you wonder.

"Woe to me!" you cry. Then out of your mouth comes a confession of sin and an admission of guilt that has been weighing upon you for years. It has been blocking your fellowship with God. You know that now. You know why you feel the need to confess. "My eyes have seen the King, the Lord Almighty," you explain. No further elucidation is required.

You watch as one of the angels leaves the throne room, approaches the fire on the altar, removes with tongs a live coal and starts coming toward you. *What's he going to do?* you wonder.

You don't have to wait long for an answer. He takes the coal and touches your lips. You hear a sizzle and smell burning flesh, but strangely you have never felt better in your life. Your sin has been forgiven and your mouth has been consecrated to God.

So when the voice of the Lord booms from the throne, asking for someone to be His spokesman, you are quick to answer, "Here am I, Lord. Send me!"

The sovereign Lord takes you up on your offer. He entrusts you with a ministry that will be a hard one, but what choice do you have but to serve Him? You are thankful God has allowed you to glimpse His majestic holiness, for that is what has given you the boldness to offer your life in His service, and that is what will keep you going for many years to come.[4]

Become James, a Disciple of Jesus

Along with Peter and John, you have been invited by the Master to accompany Him to the top of a mountain to pray. You go. As you are praying, suddenly you feel the need to look up. *Something is happening to Jesus. His face is glowing. Why, it's getting brighter by the minute! Even His clothes are dazzling! What's going on?* You rise from your knees and move away.

Just then two other figures appear on the mountain. They, too, are dressed in "glorious splendor." You recognize them as two of your deceased forefathers: Moses, the lawgiver, and Elijah, the prophet. Here they are, back on earth and engaged in lively conversation with Jesus. They are discussing the Master's "departure." It all sounds rather ominous.

Peter suggests erecting a shelter for each of your guests and one for Jesus too, but his offer gets interrupted by a bright light that suddenly appears and envelops all of you. You shield your eyes with your hand. Then you lean into the luminous cloud. You feel a warmth that is comforting. It is almost as if the Spirit of God is embracing you. *But how can that be?* you wonder.

Then you hear a voice. It is deafening as it reverberates around you. "This is my Son, whom I love," the voice declares. "Listen to Him!"

Terrified, all three of you fall facedown to the ground. *What will He tell us?* you wonder. *Will He reveal that He has come to earth to make God personal? Will He tell us that when He leaves, God will still be personal in His Spirit, whose embrace I just experienced?* You have a lot to think about, but you will save those thoughts for later. Right now you feel Jesus touching you on the shoulder.

You look up. Moses and Elijah have disappeared. You four are alone again on the mountain. You cannot speak for the others, but you know that you yourself will descend with a renewed understanding that a transcendent, holy God has stepped very personally into your life, and because of it your worship can never be the same.[5]

WHAT IS WORSHIP?

According to Dr. Jonathan Bosse, pastor of New Jersey's New Monmouth Baptist Church, worship is "a celebration of God's worth." God's worth, when "perceived and appreciated by man" arouses "wonder, awe, fear, trust, gratitude, joy, and similar sentiments," a Bible dictionary elaborates.[6] Those are the emotions one experiences when one recognizes God for who He is.

Keeping this in mind, let me ask you some provocative questions. What do you think would happen if churches decided to allow the Spirit of God to have His way in worship? Would cold, staid services become "looser" and warmer? Would loose, "feely" services adopt a more holy structure? What about the individual worshiper? Would he or she be like the apostle Paul, who was caught up into the "third heaven,"[7] where his experience with God was so sacred he couldn't even put it into words?

HOW AWESOME CAN WORSHIP GET?

Picture yourself, if you will, sitting in church. It is Sunday morning. The pastor is reading from Hebrews 12:

> You have not come to a mountain that can be touched and that is burning with fire; to darkness, gloom and storm; to a trumpet blast or to such a voice speaking words that those who heard it begged that no further word be spoken to them,

because they could not bear what was commanded: "If even an animal touches the mountain, it must be stoned." The sight was so terrifying that Moses said, "I am trembling with fear."

But you have come to Mount Zion, to the heavenly Jerusalem, the city of the living God. You have come to thousands upon thousands of angels in joyful assembly, to the church of the firstborn, whose names are written in heaven. You have come to God, the judge of all men, to the spirits of righteous men made perfect, to Jesus the mediator of a new covenant, and to the sprinkled blood that speaks a better word than the blood of Abel.

Therefore, since we are receiving a kingdom that cannot be shaken, let us be thankful, and so worship God acceptably with reverence and awe, for our "God is a consuming fire" (vv. 18-24,28,29).

As you follow along in your Bible, you are reminded again that the reverential fear that past saints experienced is meant to be part of your own worship this morning. Because you live on this side of the cross, however, Jesus Christ will wrap your awe in joyful love.

When you entered the sanctuary a few moments ago, you were really entering "Mount Zion," the Bible tells you. You came into "the heavenly Jerusalem, the city of the living God."

You are now approaching Jehovah, "the judge of all men" and His Son, Jesus, "the mediator of a new covenant." In your company are angels, "thousands upon thousands" of them, gathered "in joyful assembly." *I wonder how many of these celestial beings are crowded into my pew this very moment. I wish I could see their radiant faces!*

Also with you, you learn, are "spirits of the righteous made perfect." *Who are these "spirits"?* you wonder.

"[Those who] have already gone on to the heavenly regions where the angels are," suggest Bible commentators John F. Walvoord and Roy B. Zuck.[8]

As strange as it may seem, you may, then, be worshiping with your deceased loved ones: your recently departed mother, your long-gone father, the spouse you miss terribly and the baby you never had a chance to hug. Furthermore, "the whole communion of saints, the church on earth and in heaven,"[9] as commentator Frank Gaebelein calls this group, is being instructed to "worship God acceptably with reverence and awe."

These last words pierce your soul. You suddenly realize that regardless of what kind of church service you are attending, your personal worship must meet God's criteria. You are to worship Him in a way that honors His transcendent holiness, yet embraces the warmth of His personal presence.

Are there any suggestions to help you?

Yes! Yes! Yes!

Here they are:

- Be bold enough to stand before your sovereign Lord, but remember to "take off your shoes," for underneath your feet is holy ground.
- Be bold enough to approach the throne of grace at any time of the day or night, knowing the King will extend His scepter, but remember the price that was paid to grant you entrance into His private chamber. It was the blood of His only Son.
- Be bold enough to offer your sacrifice in heaven's "holy of holies," but expect to get goose bumps when you gaze upon your Savior's face. For you are witnessing the firstfruits of what will be an everyday occurrence once you join your departed loved ones in glory.
- Be bold enough to address any member of the Trinity, but remember to respect each one's title: God the Father, God the Son and God the Holy Spirit. They are the Three-in-One, and all are "holy, holy, holy."
- Be bold enough to ask the Lord your most bothersome questions, but realize your Teacher may not always answer to your satisfaction. His ways are "past finding out."
- Be bold enough to present in prayer your most intimate requests, but be careful to submit all desires to the Master's will. He sees the bigger picture and has a plan that is perfect.
- Be bold enough to accept whatever the Lord gives you, but don't forget to thank Him for whatever you receive, good or bad. For everything has a redeeming purpose.
- Be bold enough to run to your heavenly Father and take refuge in His outstretched arms, but remember His embrace is a holy one. You are being loved by God Himself.

These are some suggestions for worshiping God with a boldness that respects His holiness and, therefore, ushers us into His presence "acceptably."

What an incredible experience worship can be, you think. *And it's all made possible by the Lord Jesus Christ, who opened the way into the "Most Holy Place" by shedding His own blood. Therefore, I can "draw near to God with a sincere heart in full assurance of faith."* [10]

One thing is bothering you, though. You know that once you leave your "sanctuary" and present yourself to the world, people should be able to tell that you have been with God. The question is, How do you let them know? How do you "live Christ"?

The Holy Spirit has an answer. Read on.

Notes

1. This story is based on the book of Esther.
2. This account is a compilation of Moses' encounters with God as described in Exodus 19, 20, 33, 34 and Hebrews 12:29.
3. This account is based on the regulations specified in Exodus 19:24 and Leviticus 8 and 16.
4. This account is based on Isaiah's vision as described in chapter 6 of his book.
5. This account of the Transfiguration is based on a compilation of Scripture verses: Matthew 17:1-13; Mark 9:2-13; Luke 9:28-36.
6. Melancthon W. Jacobus, Edward E. Nourse and Andrew C. Zenos, *A New Standard Bible Dictionary* (New York and London: Funk and Wagnalls Company, 1926), p. 953.
7. See 2 Corinthians 12:2.
8. John F. Walvoord and Roy B. Zuck, *The Bible Knowledge Commentary* (Wheaton, Ill.: Victor Books, 1983), p. 811.
9. Frank E. Gaebelein, *The Expositor's Bible Commentary*, Vol. 12 (Grand Rapids: Zondervan Publishing House, 1981), p. 142.
10. Hebrews 10:19-22.

6

A Fitting Lifestyle

Do you not know that your body is a temple of the Holy
Spirit, who is in you,...Therefore honor God with your body.
1 CORINTHIANS 6:19,20

It is reported that one day Alexander the Great, king of Macedonia, heard
rumors that one of his troops was being delinquent in his military duties,
so he called the recruit before him.

"Soldier," the commander boomed, "some disturbing reports are cir-
culating about your conduct. Tell me, are they true?"

"Yes, sir," the soldier answered, swallowing hard.

"I guess you know I'm disappointed in you."

"Yes, sir. I am sorry, sir."

"For the record, soldier, what is your name?"

"My name is Alexander, sir."

"Alexander? You bear the name Alexander!?"

"Yes, sir."

"Well, young man, I have one thing to say to you: either change your
conduct or change your name!"

IS THERE A SPIRITUAL LESSON?

Yes. Once we become Christians through faith in the Lord Jesus Christ,
we are children of the King and are expected to bear our Monarch's name

with dignity. After all, the word "Christian" means "Christ-one." It means we are representatives of the Savior Himself.

Leon Morris, an Australian author, in his book *The Atonement*, gives this idea of representing God a personal touch. He likens God's union with Israel to the wedding of a prince to a commoner. He has the groom say to his bride, "My dear, you have become a member of the royal family. You are royalty. It is important that you live as a member of the royal family should."[1]

Could not the Holy Spirit of Christ say the same to us, who are members of His Church? After all, His Church is a Royal Family. As members, we are role models, both to those within the Family and to those outside. It is a high calling. The Bible reminds us, "From everyone who has been given much, much will be demanded."[2]

If we fail in our mission, we pay a steep price. We lose fellowship with the King, we experience discord with other members of the Royal Family and we lose credibility with those outside the faith—those who are looking up to us.

Who can help us? The Holy Spirit. Before we call upon Him, however, we need to ask ourselves a question: Do we revere Him enough to obey the code of conduct He has established? According to Charles Haddon Spurgeon, nineteenth-century British preacher, "The church will never prosper until more reverently it believes in the Holy Ghost."[3] Therefore, some changes in our lifestyles may be necessary.

WHAT CHANGES ARE REQUIRED?

Changes that lead to holiness, the Bible says, are required. Changes that reflect the purity of the God who dwells within us.

That's impossible, you may be thinking. *I can't make myself holy. I can't make myself pure.*

You are right. You can't. As was pointed out earlier, though, that's where our Helper comes in. It is His job to transform us into the image of Christ. E. Stanley Jones, the missionary statesman, puts it this way: "The work of the Holy Spirit is to produce a holy spirit."[4] It might be added: The Spirit won't be satisfied until He does. His goal is a lofty one. When people look at Christians, He wants them to see Christ.

This goal behooves us, of course, to find out the specifics of what the Spirit of Christ expects. How do we do this? By studying His Word and applying it to ourselves. In it we learn we are required to yield our bodies, part by stubborn part, to the control of our Holy Resident. We have His written instructions to help us.

SOME BIBLICAL "DON'TS"

- DON'T QUENCH THE SPIRIT. Oswald Chambers notes, "The checks of the Spirit come in the most extraordinarily gentle ways, and if you are not sensitive enough to detect His voice, you will quench it, and your personal spiritual life will be impaired."[5]

What does it mean to "quench" the Spirit? Greek scholars tell us it means "to stifle, to suppress, to restrain," and, simply, "to put out the Spirit's fire." We do this, the Bible indicates, in the following ways:

By not responding when we feel the Spirit's nudges—nudges to share our faith, to read the Bible, to pray, to go to church, to make public our commitment to Christ or to follow our Savior in baptism.

We also quench the Spirit in several other ways:

1. By not using the gifts the Spirit has given us or by keeping others from using theirs;
2. Not respecting our spiritual leaders;
3. Sowing seeds of discord among our brothers and sisters in the faith;
4. Withholding encouragement from those who need it;
5. Retaliating when we have been wronged;
6. Wallowing in depression;
7. Neglecting our prayer life;
8. Forgetting to thank God when He has blessed us;
9. Stifling the preaching of God's Word;
10. Rushing ahead in our decisions without consulting God's Word;
11. Dabbling in evil;
12. Taking credit for what the Holy Spirit is doing in us and through us;

13. Acting contrary to the lifestyle that is expected to accompany the royal title "Christian."[6]

• DON'T GRIEVE THE SPIRIT. Charles Haddon Spurgeon gives a reason for this admonition. "Anything we do that grieves the Spirit of God must take away from us some part of our power for good,"[7] he says. How frightening! To grieve can also be translated "to pain, to distress, to offend," even "to vex." Now, what are some of the specific actions that grieve the Holy Spirit? The Bible mentions quite a list:

1. Indulging in impurity;
2. Harboring resentment;
3. Being greedy;
4. Verbally tearing apart those we love;
5. Giving in to bitterness;
6. Rage;
7. Anger;
8. Brawling;
9. Slander;
10. Malice;
11. Sensuality;
12. Deceit;
13. Lying;
14. Stealing;
15. Gutter talk;
16. Drunkenness.[8]

Any of these things make it uncomfortable for the Spirit to be our "Houseguest," so He retreats to a corner and weeps. He is not only sad, but He is also "vexed." He asks, "Why? Why are you offending Me? Why are you mocking My standards? Don't you want Me here? When you gave your life to Christ, you agreed you needed a new beginning. You were given that. Past sins were washed away. All things were made new. What happened? Why did you revert to your old ways? Why are you living like a pagan? Don't you realize the Christian life is a changed life? The apostle Peter says, 'But just as he who called you is holy, so be holy in all you do.'"[9]

How do you think the Spirit feels when He tells us to stop participating in a particular practice and we pay Him no heed? Or when we are inattentive, even disrespectful, during a formal worship service? Or when we profane our bodies, His personal temple, by giving various parts of those bodies (minds, eyes, ears, mouths, hearts, hands, feet or reproductive parts) over to evil? Or when we desecrate His Word by adding to it, detracting from it, changing its meaning, saying it contains errors, swearing on it in court, then testifying falsely, throwing it across the room in a fit of anger, or just plain neglecting it? Don't you imagine He is grieved?

- DON'T LIE TO THE SPIRIT. Ananias and Sapphira found this out the hard way. Their sin of pretense cost them their lives. Apparently, they wanted to "fit in" with other believers who were selling their land or houses and giving the money to the poor. So they sold their own property and collected the money. When they laid the proceeds at the apostles' feet, however, the offering wasn't complete. They held some back.

As Peter told them, their sin was not in what they held back (keeping a portion was their prerogative), but their sin was in making it appear they were giving the whole amount. The Holy Spirit, of course, knew they weren't. He was right there when the deceit took place. He may have been thinking, *If I can't trust them with money, how can I trust them with more significant things?* At any rate, He demanded their lives—and He took them.[10]

That's a rather drastic response to a mere lie, you might be thinking. Perhaps it is. It was important, though, for the Spirit of Christ to establish right from the beginning that members of Christ's Church have a standard of conduct to follow. It is high—very high indeed.

- DON'T BLASPHEME THE SPIRIT. This is called "the unforgivable sin." It attributes to Satan the works of Christ, denies Christ's authority and chooses to oppose Christ and everything He stands for—all this in the face of Holy Spirit-revealed truth. Thankfully, if we have been "born again," no sin we commit is unpardonable. If we have NOT been born again, however, all sins condemn us. So according to the author of the book of Hebrews, the message is clear: Don't harden your heart. Today is the day of salvation. Repent of your sins and turn your life over to the control of the Holy Spirit. You may not get another chance.[11]

SOME BIBLICAL DO'S

Imagine you are back in the same room where you met the Holy Spirit through the introductions of your spiritual forefathers. You are alone. Suddenly you feel the same sensation you experienced before, right after Christ left the room and the Holy Spirit came in. You can't put your finger on why, but the atmosphere in the room has changed. You can't see anyone or hear any audible sound, yet you know Someone has entered. He comes close and asks if He may speak personally.

Let Him. Let the Spirit of God speak through His Word to your heart. Remember why He is being so thorough in His instructions: He wants to make you "holy."

This time He skips any introductory remarks and gets to the core of the matter. "Rely on Me to do what is right for you," the Spirit begins. "Trust Me with all your heart, lean not on your own understanding; in all your ways acknowledge Me, and I will make your paths straight.

"My guidance will come through the Bible," the Spirit continues, "the Word I breathed into human authors. You will find it useful for teaching, rebuking, correcting and training in righteousness so that you may be thoroughly equipped for every good work.

"Whenever you approach My Word, though, remember to be receptive to what it has to say. Let My teaching fall like rain and My Word descend like dew, like showers on new grass, like abundant rain on tender plants. But understand that the same Word that nourishes you may sometimes hurt you. For it is a two-edged sword, penetrating, dividing and judging. But any hurt you feel is always for your ultimate good, for I care about you.

"Also, receive the gifts I give you, and do so gratefully, not coveting that which I have bestowed upon someone else. For I give gifts to each one just as I determine. For each individual the gift is right.

"Remember, too, to confess your sins daily. That's how you keep the house you've invited Me to live in clean. If you confess your sins, Christ is faithful and just and will forgive your sins and purify you from all unrighteousness.

"If you are ever on trial for your faith, I have an encouraging word for you then as well. Ask Me to help you prepare your defense. I will give you words that none of your adversaries will be able to resist or contradict. I promise.

"Whenever you are hurting, publicly or privately, let Me hold you. Let Me draw you close to My heart—so close you can feel the beat of My love, so close you can hear My gentle whisper: 'I love you, I love you, I love you!' For as a mother comforts her child, so will I comfort you.

"Now, a word about your future. Always be open to the 'more' I have for you. Be willing to go deeper. Forget the past. Concentrate on what is ahead. Strain to reach the end of the race and receive the prize for which God is calling you up to heaven.

"Life will continue to present challenges. There's only one way to handle them and come out on top. You've got to be willing to risk everything for your Lord: defeat, danger, even death. But be assured, whatever comes, My grace is sufficient for you.[12]

"My last remark is a plea, from My heart to yours. So listen carefully. Friend, when I came into your life, I came in fully. You have all of Me. But I don't have all of you. I want to immerse you, to control every part of you: your walk, your prayer life, your outreach, your desires, your thoughts—all of you. For then you will be able to carry out My other instructions effortlessly. They will be as natural for you as breathing.

"I hope that by now you know you can trust Me. I have been faithful to other believers, and I will be faithful to you. I have blessings already prepared for you to enjoy, but in order to receive them, you must step into the water. So now is the time to ask you the big question: Are you ready to accompany Me to the river?"

"Yes," you answer, "I am. I'm ready to put what I've learned into practice. When I get to the water, though, I hope I can do what is expected of me because, you see, I have a question that keeps bothering me: How far can I go without drowning?"

Notes

1. Leon Morris, *The Atonement* (Downers Grove, Ill.: InterVarsity Press, 1963), p. 26.
2. Luke 12:48.
3. Charles Haddon Spurgeon, *Spurgeon's Morning and Evening* (Grand Rapids: Zondervan Publishing House, 1965), p. 95, quoted by Swindoll, p. 263.
4. E. Stanley Jones, *Selections from E. Stanley Jones* (Nashville: Abingdon Press, 1944), p. 250.
5. Oswald Chambers, *My Utmost for His Highest* (New York: Dodd, Mead, and Company, 1935), p. 226.
6. This section is based on 1 Thessalonians 5.

7. Charles Haddon Spurgeon, *The Soul Winner* (Grand Rapids: Wm. B. Eerdmans Publishing Company, 1963), p. 283.

8. This section is based on Ephesians 4:17—5:28.

9. First Peter 1:15.

10. This section is based on Acts 4:32—5:11.

11. This section is based on Matthew 12:22-37 and Hebrews 3:7-19.

12. This section is based on the following Scripture references: Proverbs 3:5,6; 2 Timothy 3:16; Deuteronomy 32:2; Hebrews 4:12; 1 Corinthians 12:11; 1 John 1:9; Luke 21:15; Isaiah 66:13; Philippians 3:13 *(TLB)*; 2 Corinthians 12:9.

PART TWO:
A Progressive Immersion

[For my determined purpose is] that I may know
Him [that I may progressively become more deeply
and intimately acquainted with Him].
PHILIPPIANS 3:10 *(AMP.)*

Covering the Feet
(Our Christian Walk)

Keep in step with the Spirit.
GALATIANS 5:25

You are at the edge of the river—the same river you imagined yourself standing beside at the beginning of this book. You are listening to the lap of the waves at the shoreline and to the rush of the current farther out. You are wondering, more seriously than ever, if you should join your guide, a more mature Christian who has offered to be your mentor. Right now he is beckoning from the water.

As you stand on the beach, you feel tuned in to the river's spiritual significance. It symbolizes the flow of God's Spirit through the ages. You are being invited to become part of this segment of it. *Amazing!* You must hesitate no longer, though, for the river will continue to move on, with or without you. *That's scary!*

"Enter the flow," Frances Roberts says. "It is the flow of divine life....Labor, learn, attempt to live apart from its power and impetus, and all is ultimately weariness of body, frustration of soul, disappointment of heart, and failure in purpose."[1] *I'm ready to move* on *to better things,* you remind yourself. *So...*

WHAT ARE MY INSTRUCTIONS?

Remember what your driving instructor told you to do when you come to an intersection? STOP, LOOK, LISTEN, then GO! The same directions apply when you come to a spiritual decision point. First, STOP. Come away from your daily routine and just be still. Don't "do" anything; contemplate. Concentrate on the fact that the Spirit is God, that He is with you at this very moment, and that He loves you. Relax in His everlasting arms. Feel His heartbeat.

After a sufficient time, LOOK. Look around and within. Examine your life for areas in which you might have a greater influence for Christ. How about your family relationships? Your work environment? Your neighborhood? Your church involvement? Can you let the Spirit minister through you in an area without getting in His way?

Before you jump into an activity that is new, however, examine your abilities. In what areas has God's Spirit supernaturally equipped you to serve? Do you like to be "up front," leading singing or conducting meetings? Or are you more of a behind-the-scenes person?

Maybe you have the gift of vision and can clearly see the direction your organization should go. Perhaps you are a good listener, considering it a privilege to bear another's burdens. Or maybe you have the gift of discernment. Or teaching. Or encouragement. Or the ability to speak to listeners about Jesus Christ in a "language" they can understand.

What about the gift of "helps," which equips a person to do whatever needs to be done? Or the flair for hospitality, warmly opening heart and home? Or the supernatural knack of touching hurting lives with the healing power of God? Or the gift of prayer, which perseveres on behalf of those in need? Then, too, consider on-the-go spiritual endowments, such as evangelism, conference speaking and missionary outreach. The abilities with which the Spirit may have blessed you have no end.

So LISTEN. The Spirit will communicate His desires. Charles Stanley in *The Wonderful Spirit-Filled Life* elaborates by saying, "To walk by the Spirit is to live with moment-by-moment dependency on and sensitivity to the initial promptings of the Holy Spirit. It is a lifestyle."[2] So learn to cup your spiritual ears in such a way that they will stay cupped, so that when the Spirit says, "This is the way; walk in it," you will hear Him.

It is one of the Spirit's functions to sort through needs and opportunities, then match one or more of them with the abilities with which He has gifted us. It is His job to let us know where He wants to use us. As He makes His assessment, He takes into consideration the desire of our hearts, for He knows the match will be made more easily if our desires match His. To make sure they do, we must be faithful in our Bible reading. For the Spirit usually "speaks" by practically applying biblical principles. Once we receive His message and its rightness is confirmed in our hearts, we are to hesitate no longer.

> We must stop doing what we
> have always done in the way
> we have always done it. It is
> time to move out of "neutral."

GO! Easier said than done? I identify. When I was a teenager, neatness was not a priority. I had the sloppy habit of leaving my shoes, slippers and boots strewn in disarray all over my bedroom carpet. When warnings were not enough to convince me to tidy up, my father decided to take creative action. One day I opened my door to a sight that made me laugh out loud. There on the floor was my footwear, arranged like footprints leading from one side of the room to the other. By placing my feet in one foot covering at a time, I could "walk" across the bedroom floor without ever touching the rug.

This is the way Spirit walking is supposed to be, the experts tell us. "We find that each step has been prepared for us," F. B. Meyer says, "so that we have but to put down our feet."[3] Walking in the Spirit, however, doesn't seem so easy to us "ordinary" Christians. Why? Maybe it would help if we heeded some practical answers to a very practical question:

HOW DO WE LEARN TO WALK?

J. S. Bunting states, "Progress in any direction demands that in some sense we quit the place where we are [STOP]. If we put one foot forward, we must lift one foot from the ground."[4] That means we must stop doing what we have always done in the way we have always done it. It is time to move out of "neutral."

Next, reprioritize activities [LOOK]. In doing so, we may find that the Saturday golf game is slipping in importance. Or the bathrooms will have to be cleaned on Tuesday instead of Monday. Or, horror of horrors, we have to give up one God-glorifying activity for another. These changes will not be easy. According to Henry T. Blackaby and Claude V. King, the best-selling authors of *Experiencing God*, "Any time you go from where you are to where God is working, from your way of thinking to God's way of thinking, from your ways to God's ways, or from your purpose to His purpose [LISTEN], a major adjustment will be required."[5]

The greatest challenge of all, however, can be giving up control. We like to place our own shoes on our own precharted course. Once we give up plotting our own moves, though, a glorious release comes. Listen to what happened to a friend of V. Raymond Edman: "What once had been painful trying had become perfect trusting. Weakness had been turned into strength, sighing into song, and total failure into triumph—all because he learned to be filled with the Holy Spirit and to walk in the Spirit [GO!]."[6]

WHAT ARE INDICATORS I AM WALKING IN THE SPIRIT?

Your life will be integrated when you are walking in the Spirit. No longer will you compartmentalize your religion. Your Christianity will cease to be like rich cream at the top of an old-fashioned glass milk bottle, served on Sunday, leaving a watery substance for the rest of the week. Rather, it will be "homogenized" into your dailiness, so effectively, in fact, that people will see Christ in your every action. What a change!

You will also feel confident traveling routes that are unfamiliar. "I will lead the blind by ways they have not known," the Spirit predicts; "along unfamiliar paths I will guide them."[7] So you will not be discouraged when you enter unfamiliar territory and even do so "blindly." Your inability to see the end of the road will make you more sensitive to the Spirit's nudges.

You will also be content to advance one step at a time. Before, that would not have been fast enough. Now, you know the Christian walk is meant to be slow going. You also know you will eventually arrive at your destination. "The Almighty is tedious," F. B. Meyer reminds us, "but He is sure."[8]

SOME THINGS OF WHICH TO BE AWARE

The Spirit does not always signal changes in direction. That's why it is important to stay close by His side. Walking in the Spirit is like what a dog does when it "heels." It keeps its right eye focused on its master's left knee. That way it can tell instantly when the master is about to do something different, like turn left, bear right or stop. The concentration involved can indeed be "tedious," but walking "in sync" permits us to visit places we couldn't otherwise go. It also protects us from the dangers of wandering.

> The way God leads may not be the way we would choose to go. Rarely does the Spirit travel the shortest route.

Another alert: The way God leads may not be the way we would choose to go. For example, rarely does the Spirit travel the shortest route. Remember how long it took the Israelites to go through the wilderness? We, too, may endure years of wondering why we are where we are, doing what we are doing, before we finally enter "the promised land."

In our spiritual journey we should also expect difficulties. If the Israelites' blood pressure didn't rise when Pharaoh's army was pounding at their heels, it probably did when the Amalekites (and some other "ites") attacked them. It surely did when they came to an oasis and found the water polluted. They faced dangers, fights and disappointments. Rare is the Christian who would program them into his or her Christian experience. The Spirit is different from us though. So when we encounter problems, it is a sure sign we are being led by Someone whose ways are higher than ours.

Then, too, we should expect to be overcome at times by an intense feeling of aloneness. When we are, it helps to understand that feeling and fact are often in opposition. So we reach for the Word. That contains fact. "Never will I leave you," the Author whispers, "never will I forsake you."[9] He is commanding a great company of believers—a company that will take hits and will sustain wounds. As a unit, though, it will advance and conquer. Our spiritual journey is not without challenges, but we are assured we are not traveling all by ourselves.

SOME MARCHING ORDERS

It helps to pay close attention to our Commanding General. Some of His directions are expected. Others surprise us. For example, "Forward, march!" is a given. "Halt" is not.

> When the water of God's
> Spirit covers our feet, love
> will cover our walk.

Consider what happened to Amy Carmichael, faithful missionary in India who, during her years of service, suffered a crippling fall. It stopped her in the midst of her work—stopped her for 20 years. In that time of inactivity, however, she experienced great blessings. In her book *His Thoughts Said, His Father Said*, she "hears" the Holy Spirit say, "Stand still....Give Me time to bathe thee in peace."[10] It was a message that breathed significance into a seemingly meaningless situation. She had to be listening, though, to receive it.

Occasionally, we hear the Spirit shout, "About face!" This is essentially what Abraham heard as he was racing ahead of God by trying to produce the child of promise through his servant Hagar rather than through his wife, Sarah. As a result of his disobedience, he had to go back to square one and start over.

Christian "soldiers" don't choose the commands they receive. They are expected to obey the ones that are given. This is not only for their own good, but also for the benefit of the whole army. I know this is heavy stuff, but it is important.

"When people look at God's army," you may ask, "what should they see?"

Love
When the water of God's Spirit covers our feet, love will cover our walk. What we demonstrate to others will have the characteristics of the love God pours out to us. For starters, this Christlike love will be lasting, pure, free, unconditional, forgiving and boundless, the Bible says. It will also be "very patient and kind, never jealous or envious, never boastful or proud, never haughty or selfish or rude."[11] Tell me, does this kind of love sound like something we are capable of producing in and of ourselves?

Of course not. It is ours, though, once we let the water of God's Spirit come up to our ankles.

Light
Spirit walkers also manifest an inner glow—a spiritual luminance that comes from being at peace with God, with themselves and with others. They shine, like Moses, with the Lord's presence.

"Really?" you may question. "Then why is it so many Christians I know look like they've been baptized in pickle juice?"

They are quenching the Spirit of Jesus, who clearly commanded, "Let your light shine before men, that they may see your good deeds and praise your Father in heaven."[12]

We are not finished describing Christlike characteristics yet. In a genuine Spirit walker, observers will also see...

Humility
"And what does the Lord require of you?" asks Micah, the prophet. Then he answers, "To act justly and to love mercy and to walk humbly with your God."[13]

Remember King Nebuchadnezzar of Babylon? One day he strutted out onto his balcony, looked down upon his city and proudly declared, "Is not this the great Babylon I have built, by my mighty power and for the glory of my majesty?"

Nebuchadnezzar, you remember, ended up losing touch with reality and found himself groveling on the ground, eating grass with the beasts. How humiliating! God in His mercy, however, drenched the king with "the dew of heaven." This refreshment from the Spirit is what brought him back to his senses and caused him to give credit where credit was due. "Now I, Nebuchadnezzar," he proclaimed in the end, "praise and exalt and glorify the King of heaven."[14]

So any time we are tempted to feel we have made it on our own, it may help to remember this example. You see, every knee will eventually bow to the One who makes all things possible. It is just easier to bow early on.

LEARNING TO AVOID ROADBLOCKS

As we begin our walk with the Spirit, it is wise to watch for hindrances. One is THE TUG OF THE WORLD. Joni Eareckson Tada speaks for all of us when she says, "I'm tired of prying the world's suction cups off my heart!"[15]

Her words remind us of the rich young ruler of biblical fame. When Jesus told him that in order to inherit eternal life, he would have to give up what he loved best—the world's goods—he went away sorrowful.

This kind of sorrow, however, is not the only kind that hinders spiritual progress. Sorrow about LEAVING FAMILY can be another. Though family ties are high on God's list of priorities, they are never to be above the divine claim on a life. Perhaps that is why Jesus said, "Anyone who loves his father or mother more than me is not worthy of me; anyone who loves his son or daughter more than me is not worthy of me." The Spirit of God wants—and deserves—our total commitment.

A third hindrance is MAGNETISM TO THE PAST. It gives us second thoughts when the Spirit calls. Jesus warned, "'No one who puts his hand to the plow and looks back is fit for service in the kingdom of God.'"

The writer of the book of Hebrews adds, "Let us throw off everything that hinders."[16]

Having these words in mind, it seems to me there is no better time for you, the reader, to "unload" than right now. Do you agree? Are you ready to get rid of things that will undoubtedly weigh you down once you are in the "water"?

THE QUESTION PENETRATES

The Lord has spoken. You know it is now or never; therefore, you search your heart. In it you discover enough weights to drown you: resentments, fears, hurts, anxieties, lusts and much more tonnage. Prayerfully you reach in and, one by one, you extract the weights. Then, one at a time, you hurl them as far out into the river as you can. Plop! Plop! Plop! They sink. Then the water covers each burial spot and continues its onward flow to the sea.

Whew! I'm free. Now it's time. Gingerly you lift your foot and immerse it in the water. *Oooh!* The cold makes you shiver.

"You'll get used to it," your mentor reassures you. "In fact, most people who get their feet wet want to come in all the way."

"Really?" you ask as the water laps around your ankles. "All the way?"

Notes

1. Frances Roberts, *Come Away My Beloved* (Ojai, Calif.: King's Farspan, Inc., 1973), p. 179.
2. Charles Stanley, *The Wonderful Spirit-Filled Life* (Nashville: Thomas Nelson Publishers, 1992), p. 97.
3. F. B. Meyer, *Daily Meditations* (Dallas, Tex.: Word Books, 1979), July 26.
4. J. S. Bunting, *The Secret of a Quiet Mind* (London, England: Oliphant Ltd., 1956), p. 74.
5. Henry T. Blackaby and Claude V. King, *Experiencing God* (Nashville: Broadman and Holman Publishers, 1994), p. 151.
6. V. Raymond Edman, *They Found the Secret* (Grand Rapids: Zondervan Publishing House, 1960), p. 137.
7. Isaiah 42:16.
8. Meyer, *Daily Meditations*, September 29.
9. Hebrews 13:5.
10. Amy Carmichael, *His Thoughts Said, His Father Said* (Fort Washington, Pa.: Christian Literature Crusade, n.d.), p. 38.
11. First Corinthians 13:4 *(TLB)*.
12. Matthew 5:16.
13. Micah 6:8.
14. See Daniel 4:28-37.
15. Joni Eareckson Tada, quoted by Dave Goetz in "Joni's Confession," 1996, *Christianity Today*, Inc./*Christian Reader* 34, no. 3 (May/June 1996): 12.
16. The section is based on the following Scripture verses: Matthew 10:37; Luke 9:62; Hebrews 12:1.

8

Covering the Knees (Our Prayer Life)

And God heard them, for their prayer reached
heaven, his holy dwelling place.

2 CHRONICLES 30:27

As you stand in the water, which is lapping around your ankles, your wise Christian guide repeats his invitation to come in deeper. "Up to your knees!" he urges. "Let the Spirit cover your prayer life."

Your thoughts fly back to your dying mother's bedside. Family members have gathered in her room in the nursing home. The mood is somber. Through your tears you try to assess the situation: *How should I pray: "Lord, take her to heaven" or "Lord, restore her to health"?*

Your problem back then was knowing God's will. It still is. *Wouldn't it be wonderful,* you muse, *to have someone who prays correctly do my interceding for me?* Then it hits you. *That's what my mentor is trying to tell me. I do have an Intercessor: God's Holy Spirit! If I turn my prayer life over to Him, He will "cover" me, even during those times when I pray amiss.*

As you are trying to grasp this concept of having your "knees covered with water," you find yourself grappling and doing so for the first time really with...

THE TRUE NATURE OF PRAYER

How should one define prayer? Is it simply a Christian obligation and only that? In other words, does God expect us to recite the Lord's Prayer at least once a day, say grace before every meal, then at bedtime ask Him to bless our family, our church, our nation and our missionaries around the world and think we have truly prayed?

If so, it may be wise to ask ourselves some probing questions. For instance, is prayer a ritual or a relationship? Does prayer earn brownie points with God? Who initiates prayer? Do we, or does God?

Let me offer a suggestion. Instead of thinking of prayer as a human attempt to persuade God to do our will, think of it as God burdening His people to accomplish His will. An exciting switch, isn't it? Once we grasp its truth, we will find ourselves exchanging our "Gimmes" for "Glorify Your name." Now I must admit, praying like this doesn't come naturally, not to me or to anyone else I know. It does, however, come supernaturally once we open ourselves to the Holy Spirit's leading.

Prayer begins in the mind of God. God entrusts His burden to one or more Christians. The Christians, in turn, lift the burden as a petition. The petition, then, returns as an answer. The answer is acknowledged with praise to the Lord, who started the process in the first place. Who facilitates this downward-upward flow? God's Holy Spirit. "The Spirit conveys the will of God to the saints," F. B. Meyer explains, "and bears back their prayers to God."[1] The Spirit is an active Agent, and His actions involve us.

You may have a hard time understanding what God could possibly want with simple human prayers. So do I, but I know that God, in His infinite wisdom, has decreed to use them. In fact, without them, a link in the divine chain of events would be missing. Every prayer is important, and every Christian who prays, critical. For the pray-er is God's connection between heaven and earth. He or she is an integral part of what God is about.

How does all this affect us? This way: Every time we feel burdened, we drop to our knees. Why? Because we know from where the burden is probably coming. So we form a petition. Then we wait. Are we interpreting God's will accurately? What will happen? Excitement mounts.

BIBLICAL PRAYERS

For those of you who like to recite memorized prayers and do so regularly, let me encourage you to keep it up, especially when it comes to the Lord's Prayer. You can't find a more beautiful expression of praise and petition anywhere. It comes directly from the mind of the Savior.

It is not the only biblical prayer, however, that lends itself to recitation. You may want to explore some other prayers in the Bible—some of which can be personalized simply by inserting the names of loved ones in appropriate places. You will find these Scripture-prayers so compact that in a few words you will be able to say just about everything that is on your heart—and say it well.

For example, Philippians 1:9,10 may be prayed as follows: "And this is my prayer: that [Judy's] love may abound more and more in knowledge and depth of insight, so that [she] may be able to discern what is best and may be pure and blameless until the day of Christ."

On behalf of your children, you may select John 17:9,11, which will go something like this: "I am not praying for the world, but for [Dirk, Greg and Jeff] whom you have given me, for they are yours....Holy Father, protect them by the power of your name." It is exciting to think that you can pray for your loved ones the same way Jesus prayed for His, and realize the Holy Spirit could give you both the same words.

The most exciting change you will notice is that every time you pray, you will experience deeper...

COMMUNION WITH GOD

The One who used to be a mere Acquaintance will have become your trusted Friend. You will find yourself wanting to chat with Him frequently, expressing your deepest feelings. "Holy Father," your heart will cry, "I just want to praise You." Or, "Gracious Lord, I blew it; I am sorry." Or, "O God, how grateful I am that You care!" Or, "Lord, I love You. Oh, how I love You!"

Can you see what we have here? Two kinds of praying. We have formal prayers, recited at scheduled times, as well as spontaneous outbursts, freely expressed anytime, anywhere. Sometimes it is a combination of both. God looks forward to all these prayers.

We must never discount the times we set aside for the sole purpose of talking things over with Him. Just as He sent His cloud of glory to stand guard at the entrance of Moses' "tent of meeting,"[2] so you can be sure He sends His Spirit to protect the doors of our prayer closets. That is how precious these times of interaction are to Him.

To make them precious to you as well, you may want to do what I do: Organize your praises and petitions in a series of concentric circles. Starting with your own needs, proceed to your family's needs, then on to the needs of your friends, your church, your nation and your world. Last, mention missionaries serving around the world and enclose them in a blanket of God's love. If you follow this pattern every day, you will find you can pick up where you leave off in case you are interrupted.

> Prayer is relationship, fellowship and communion——a moment-by-moment awareness of the Lord who is beside us, with us and in us.

Once you exit your "prayer closet," though, you are not finished praying. You are now free to practice what the Spirit calls "continuous prayer."[3] You see, as we become more and more comfortable in the Spirit's presence, we are more apt to listen than to speak, more willing to commune than to communicate, more content to be still and know that He is God.

John Bunyan, the seventeenth-century British preacher, is reported to have said, "In prayer, it is better to have a heart without words than words without a heart." He grasped prayer's true essence, which is more than talking to God (praising, confessing, thanking and requesting)—much more. It is relationship, fellowship and communion—a moment-by-moment awareness of the Lord who is beside us, with us and in us. It is two hearts beating as one. It is divinity and humanity working in concert.

As part of this close communion, some Christians want to know if it is ever okay to ask for...

SIGNS FROM GOD

Some people believe it is okay to ask for signs from God and do so on occasion. In the final analysis, however, asking for physical confirmation can be a rather weak way to pray, especially if we have already received a divine directive.

Consider Gideon, whom God chose to lead a battle against the Midianites. Gideon couldn't process the information he was hearing, or he didn't want to. So he asked for a sign, three signs in fact. God in His grace honored all three, including two that involved a sheepskin. "Rain dew upon the fleece but keep the ground dry," Gideon prayed. God did so. Not satisfied, Gideon prayed again. "Rain dew upon the ground but keep the fleece dry," he requested. Again God honored his request.[4] He met this insecure pray-er right where he was. Amazing!

One time I, too, asked for a sign. A corporation-initiated transfer for my husband was in the offing, and I didn't know if he should take it. Lee had peace about it. I didn't. So I asked God to show me His will in a physical, obvious way. "If we can sell our present home and buy a new one for the same price," I told God, "I will know, then, we are supposed to move. If we can't, I will take it that we should reconsider."

I was on a shaky spiritual limb. I knew it, Lee knew it and God knew it, but guess what? God honored my request. Not only did He honor it, but also through the buyer's assuming a financial obligation we thought was ours, He did so down to the very penny. Incredible!

Now, many years later, I feel bad that I asked for that sign. God was showing us His will through the transfer itself. That was hard to see at the time, though. Once we moved, however, He confirmed His will in many wonderful ways. In our new situation we were offered opportunities for spiritual growth and outreach that would never have been afforded us in our previous location. Even if that had not been the case and we had "misread" God's will, we were still secure within His hands, for He promises to work all things for the ultimate good of His children—even their mistakes. I know that now. I'm fail safe in His love.

This incident brings to mind another question Christians sometimes ask:

HOW CONCERNED IS
GOD ABOUT DETAILS?

It is easy to become annoyed when someone in a prayer meeting requests prayer for Aunt Tillie's bunion. We sit there thinking surely more important things need to be prayed about, things such as loved ones who have cancer, marriages in the process of breaking up, relatives in the armed forces, children being abused, businesses on the verge of bankruptcy, and some might add, newly licensed teenagers who are at that very moment driving their friends around town. Now these are situations that require intercession! But Aunt Tillie's bunion?

> Once we submit our prayer life
> to the Spirit's control...we find
> that nothing seems to be too
> small (or too large) to be
> mentioned. The Bible says,
> "In EVERYTHING."

Yet we know that God is interested in little things too. Not that all of them should be mentioned in public prayer meetings. Once we submit our prayer life to the Spirit's control, however, we find that nothing seems to be too small (or too large) to be mentioned. "Do not be anxious about anything," the Spirit writes, "but in everything, by prayer and petition, with thanksgiving, present your requests to God."[5]

Did you get that? The Bible says, "In EVERYTHING."

Let's not kid ourselves, though. This verse does not mean that once we present our needs to God, we are free from situations that produce anxiety; but it does mean that we can be free from anxiety WITHIN those situations. The transfer of burdens that occurs when we pray produces in our souls...

A PEACE THAT TRANSCENDS HUMAN UNDERSTANDING

We learn how to specify each of our cares by name, then to declare, "It's yours, Lord." If for some reason a care returns (or never really leaves), we learn to release it again. We even learn to rely on the Spirit to indicate when to stop praying and when to continue with dogged persistence.

Even when we are worn out from repeatedly presenting our requests and tired of waiting for answers, we experience a certain peace. For we know the Spirit is in control. What a blessing!

The Spirit, however, gives a warning. If, for some reason or other, we decide to step out of the "water" for a while and take things back

> To stay "weightless," we have
> to keep our "knees" continually
> submerged.

under our own control, our burdens, along with our anxieties, return. To stay "weightless," we have to keep our "knees" continually submerged. As the song says, because the knee bone is connected to every other bone, an effective prayer life will be reflected by a demeanor that indicates our closeness to God. If that isn't so, we may need to make some...

LIFESTYLE ADJUSTMENTS

It is sad that some people are able to separate the way they pray from the way they live. For example, consider the religious leader who publicly asks God to bless his ministry while he is privately carrying on an adulterous affair. Deaf to biblical warnings, defensive when confronted by people who are suspicious, and deceitful when having to provide excuses for his absences, we know he must be in inner turmoil. Like King David before him, he has to be feeling as if his bones are wasting away and his strength is being sapped. Yet he makes the choice to let his sin keep drawing him back.

David, to his credit, knew what to do about his problem. "Against you, you only, have I sinned," he confessed to God. Then relief came. God forgave him, and he went back to being able to sleep at night. His lifestyle was matching his prayer life. Thus, once again he could be looked upon as a man "in whose spirit is no deceit."[6] It is the story of a beautiful restoration.

It left some innocent victims in its wake, however. It is one thing for an offender to get his or her life back in order, but what about those whose lives have been victimized? How are those people to pray?

The answer for them, as it is for all of us, is...

WITH A FORGIVING HEART

When a Christian has been wronged, he or she tends to gravitate to the imprecatory psalms, those heart cries for vengeance that could be translated, "Give it to 'em, Lord! Make 'em pay!" One of the psalmist's cries actually reads, "If only you would slay the wicked, O God!"[7] That's like praying, "Heavenly Father, kill 'em!" These are rather strong words coming from one of God's own, but they give the reader comfort in knowing that when feeling this way, he or she is not alone.

It is probably safe to say that most of us at one time or another have a desire to see an offender get what he or she deserves. What a blockade we erect, though, when we have this desire! We make it virtually impossible for the Holy Spirit to commune with the Father through us. Perhaps that is why Jesus warns, "When you stand praying, if you hold anything against anyone, forgive him, so that your Father in heaven may forgive you your sins."[8]

Forgiveness. It allows the dam between the angry Christian and his or her holy God to give way. Not only can the Christian pray again, but can also actually intercede for the one who inflicted the hurt. In some instances, the one who was wronged ends up asking God to unleash a flood of blessing upon the offender.

Is this a hard thing to do? You bet.

Is it impossible? Not with the Spirit doing the praying.

WHAT IF THE RIGHT WORDS DON'T COME?

Let the Holy Spirit form the prayer for you. Listen to how the apostle Paul describes this phenomenon:

> The Spirit helps us in our weakness. We do not know what we ought to pray for, but the Spirit himself intercedes for us with groans that words cannot express. And he...intercedes for the saints in accordance with God's will.[9]

Did you catch the import of these words? The Spirit, through the apostle, is telling us that at times our minds are so befuddled that He can't verbalize a prayer through us. So He bypasses His "channel" and goes directly to the Father. He does so with "groans that words cannot express." Therefore, we may not be aware of when the prayer goes up or the nature of the petition, but we have assurance it is being expressed correctly.

The Spirit has access to all the information available. He knows the Father's overall plan. He knows our present need. He knows that which will bring the Father the most glory. He also knows what is in our best interest. In other words, He knows the Father's will. He prays "in accordance with" that will. What a relief! Now we can release those how-do-I-pray times (such as the confusion that occurs when a loved one is critically ill) to God's Spirit, knowing He will handle them well.

OH, THE WONDER OF IT ALL!

Just think: When we pray, we are spiritually entering God's "holy of holies." We are coming "face-to-face" with our Creator. The Spirit is there to "anoint" us—to bathe us in His very presence. Once we are in a situation where this "anointing" takes place, we can never be the same. J. Wilbur Chapman, the evangelist, relates this account of praying with a certain John Hyde:

> He came to my room, turned the key in the door, dropped on his knees, waited five minutes without a single syllable coming from his lips. I could hear my own heart thumping and beating. I felt the hot tears running down my face. I knew I was with God. Then with upturned face, down which the tears were streaming, he said, "O, God!" Then for five minutes at least, he was still again, and then when he knew he was walking with God, his arm went around my shoulder and there came up from the depths of his heart such petitions for men as I had never heard before. I rose from my knees to know what real prayer was.

The author of the book who relates this account adds, "Such is a portion of the story of John Hyde, who became Praying Hyde, the man who was anointed by the Holy Spirit to pray."[10]

"I yearn for such an 'anointing,'" you confess to your guide. "I can stay in my prayer rut no longer. I have to move forward." So you lift one foot, then the other, and advance deeper into the water. Soon your knees are covered.

"Stay there a while," your leader advises. "Give yourself time to get used to God's covering. Then when you are ready to experience more of the Spirit's enablement, come in deeper. Remember, I'm here to encourage you."

Notes

1. F. B. Meyer, *Daily Meditations* (Dallas, Tex.: Word Books, 1979), October 30.
2. See Exodus 33:7-11.
3. First Thessalonians 5:16.
4. See Judges 6:36-40.
5. Philippians 4:6.
6. The section "Lifestyle Adjustments" is based on the following Scripture verses: Psalm 32:2,3,4 and Psalm 51:4.
7. Psalm 139:19.
8. Mark 11:25.
9. Romans 8:26,27.
10. V. Raymond Edman, *They Found the Secret* (Grand Rapids: Zondervan Publishing House, 1960), p. 81.

Up to the Waist
(Reproducing Our Faith)

"But you will receive power when the Holy Spirit
comes on you; and you will be my witnesses."

ACTS 1:8

Your guide has backed farther into the water. In fact, he is about as far as
he can go and still remain standing. He wants you to join him. "Up to the
waist," he urges. "Submerge the reproductive aspects of your faith. Let
God's Spirit cover your witness."

This "up-to-the-waist" segment of Ezekiel's vision reads "up to the loins"
in the *King James Version*, making clear what must be covered as we go
deeper into the Spirit. "Loins," according to the dictionary, is "the region
of strength and procreative power."

The Israelites were familiar with the command, "Gird up your loins!"
It meant, "Tuck your robe into your belt, and get ready to do battle." As
they ate their last meal (the Passover) before being freed from their

bondage in Egypt, they dined with their "loins girded," their shoes on their feet and their staffs in their hands.[1]

Why? They were ready to move forward by faith, trusting God to strengthen, preserve and multiply that faith. In turn, they would testify to His power. As they obeyed Jehovah's leading, they were aware they would have struggles along the way. In Jehovah's strength, however, they would overcome the enemy.

As Christians living in challenging times, we can identify with the Israelites. We, too, face battles. Sometimes the biggest one is with ourselves. We don't necessarily want to move out and testify. It is easier to stay put and keep silent. Perhaps that is why the psalmist prayed, "O Lord, open my lips."[2] He knew a ready tongue is the first step in a verbal witness.

We know it, too. Some of us are so reluctant to speak up, however, that for us the prayer to open our lips is incomplete. We need to add something more. My personal addition goes like this: "Trap me into testifying for You today, Lord—and make it so I can't get out of it!"

Remember this as I invite you to eavesdrop on my personal conversation with...

THE MAN ON THE PLANE

I had just taken my seat next to the window on a flight to North Carolina, where I was scheduled to speak. As I was in the process of fastening my seat belt, a man in a business suit squeezed into the seat next to mine and slid his briefcase into the space in front of his feet.

Wary of what can happen to women who travel alone, I usually don't encourage conversation with members of the opposite sex. This gentleman was a talker, though, and a passenger in such close proximity, however quiet she might be, was a listening ear.

"Which do you want?" he asked, as he was fastening his own seat belt. "The front or the back?"

"The front or the back of what?" I wondered out loud.

"The armrest," he informed me. "I like to negotiate this detail before takeoff."

"Okay," I said, "I'll take the back." That did it! He was off on a running conversation.

"Where are you going?" he queried.

"Asheville," I replied.

"Are you on vacation?" he asked, glancing at my casual attire.

"No."

"Are you on business?"

"You might call it that."

"What kind of business are you in?"

"I'm a public speaker."

He had now positioned his head so he was looking me directly in the eye. "What's your topic?" he asked.

Trapped! Divinely trapped! "The Lord Jesus Christ," I replied.

Then he became quiet. Very quiet. When he recovered, he ventured, "Have you ever heard of a group called the Gideons?"

Now it was my turn to recover. Once I did, I informed him that I was indeed familiar with this quality organization that places Bibles in hotel rooms, prisons, schools, etc.

"I ran into a Gideon last night," he told me. "He also talked about the Lord Jesus Christ."

That comment launched a conversation that kept going until we landed. As he talked, I realized this gentleman was not yet ready to place his faith in the Savior, but he was definitely being drawn in that direction. I disembarked, expecting to meet him someday in heaven. I figured that the Spirit who had placed both a Gideon and a Christian speaker in this man's path within a period of only 24 hours probably had a few more encounters for him down the road. One of them would result in his conversion, but I was embarrassed I had to be trapped into becoming a worker on the Spirit's "assembly line." Sharing Christ in a conference setting is definitely easier for me than sharing one-on-one.

Covering. That is what I need. A covering of my weaknesses with the Spirit's strength. I agree with Charles Spurgeon, who said, "The whole business [of soul winning] on our part is the height of absurdity unless we regard ourselves as used by the Holy Ghost and filled with His power."[3]

Until that happens, we are...

AT A LOSS!

Many Christians, I have learned, when presented with an opportunity to share their faith, don't know what to do. So they do nothing. Their silence causes guilt; and their guilt brings on more silence.

When asked to explain their reticence, they offer a variety of excuses. Listen and evaluate some of their comments:

- "When I was a teenager, I was confronted by a zealot who stopped me on the street and shouted, 'Sinner, are you saved?' I never got over his rudeness." (Translation: "I'm afraid I'll come on too strong.")
- "The last time I shared my faith, I got asked a question I could not answer. It was embarrassing." (Translation: "Leave evangelism to the experts.")
- "I know somebody who hands out tracts wherever she goes. Whenever she gets somebody to pray the 'Sinner's Prayer,' she chalks up a 'win' on her tally card." (Translation: "Canned approaches turn me off.")
- "I have dreams of standing before God on Judgment Day. I am watching Billy Graham receive thousands of crowns for soul winning. When it's my turn, I don't get any. I wake up in a cold sweat." (Translation: "God's quota for souls is so high no ordinary person can fill it. So why try?")

WHAT IS THE PROBLEM?

Self-absorption! All these excuses revolve around the one doing the witnessing. Too much ego is showing. No reliance is entrusted to the Holy

> The disciples realized power when they began to speak the Word of God "boldly." The same experience can be ours today.

Spirit. J. I. Packer asks a probing question: "Do we remember that the Holy Spirit alone, by His witness, can authenticate our witness, and look to Him to do so and trust Him to do so, and show the reality of our trust, as Paul did, by eschewing the gimmicks of human cleverness?"[4]

The disciples experienced this authentication by the Spirit when the following prophecy was fulfilled in their lives: "For John baptized with water, but in a few days you will be baptized with the Holy Spirit. You will receive power when the Holy Spirit comes on you; and you will be my witnesses in Jerusalem, and in all Judea and Samaria, and to the ends of the earth."[5] They realized this power when they began to speak the Word of God "boldly."[6] The same experience can be ours today. Consider...

A Farmer's Story

Imagine you are interested in growing vegetables. You select a plot, prepare your soil and plant some seed. Then you fertilize, water, weed and wait. In due time you bring in a harvest.

Growing something from start to finish is a thrill. As long as your plot of ground remains small, it is quite possible to be involved in the whole process. Once your "field" expands beyond "Jerusalem," though, and you start sowing seeds in "Judea" and beyond, you will need assistance.

Perhaps that is why the apostle Paul, who had an extensive outreach, presents witnessing as a study in cooperation. He introduces the Lord as the Owner of a "field" (the world). To bring in a harvest of souls, the Owner needs workers, whom He carefully "hires." To each worker He assigns a plot of ground, and to each He gives a "task." The worker, however, is not limited to a particular plot or task. The worker is free to go wherever the Spirit leads and to do whatever the Spirit indicates. Payment will be made, the worker is told, not according to the size of the harvest, but rather according to faithfulness in doing the task. In other words, was the job done properly?

"I planted the seed," the Scriptures say, "Apollos watered it, but God made it grow."[7]

Who "won" the soul seems relatively unimportant. It was a team effort anyway. So let's leave our tallies to God and celebrate. A brand-new Christian is a cause for rejoicing.

How refreshing this teaching is! It is like cool water being sprinkled on parched ground—on workers worn out from trying in their own efforts to increase the kingdom of God. It also gives new life to the reticent witness—the one who, for one reason or another, is reluctant to get started. Consider the principles the Spirit is presenting:

- Principle 1: No one person is responsible for "seeding" the whole world. The command "Go into all the world"[8] was given to the disciples as a group, not to any one individual. If all of us are good witnesses in our own individual "worlds" (those mission fields we work in each day or the fields to which we are led by the Holy Spirit), eventually the whole world will be "seeded" with the gospel. To speed up the process, the Spirit selects some people to be full-time missionaries, then sends them to specific mission fields.
- Principle 2: In the salvation of any one soul, more than one witnessing Christian is usually involved. Pray-ers, teachers, authors, friends and counselors—all play a part in influencing that soul for Christ. God has a whole team of workers in His mission field, and His Spirit is directing them in such a way that they are crisscrossing each other's spheres of influence daily, building upon one another's foundations.
- Principle 3: It is God who causes the seed of His gospel to "take." We can plant, we can irrigate and we can pray, but only God can cause growth. He does. Therefore, in the end He should, and He will, get the credit. The Owner of the field will have produced a harvest.

WHAT PART DOES WATER PLAY?

Water plays an invaluable part. It moistens the soil, breaks open the seed, soaks the roots, carries nutrients up the stems and washes grime off the leaves and fruit. It also prompts the plants to lift their faces to the sun, which, in concert with the water, produces a crop to make any farmer smile.

Workers need water, too. They drink and are refreshed. When they let the Spirit cover their outreach, their dry mouths disappear, their legs stop shaking and their hearts resume their steady beats. An opportunity for soul winning is presenting itself, but the symptoms that used to signal paralysis are gone. In their places are some delightful responses:

- *Anticipation.* ("I can't wait to see how the Holy Spirit is going to use me today!")

- *Excitement.* ("She seemed interested when I brought up the subject of the Lord!")
- *Amazement.* ("What a positive change has come over him in the few months we have been friends!")

> } Be "natural in spiritual things
> } and spiritual in natural things."

In words attributed to R. B. Kuiper, these Christian workers have learned to be "natural in spiritual things and spiritual in natural things."

FURTHER ENCOURAGEMENT FROM THE SCRIPTURES

King David, the author of Psalm 51, has lost spiritual credibility because of his sin with Bathsheba. He wants to get back his testimony. He yearns to be an example of God's grace, to be able to turn to someone and say with conviction, "The God who cares about me cares about you, too. Turn to Him. Learn His ways."

Before any conversions can take place in others, however, some changes have to take place in David's own life. He has to admit his guilt, appeal to God for help and abdicate his supposed "throne rights." These prerequisites are the same for us.

- *Admission of guilt.* It helps to remember we were born failing God and deserved to die for our sins. Graciously He reached down and saved us. Now that we are secure in His love, it is easy to forget our former state. It is easy to become so concerned about nurturing a good self-image that we don't realize we are still falling short of His image. We are no better, in a sense, than those we want to reach. Therefore, we can't afford to "talk down." As someone has wisely said, "Christianity is one beggar telling another beggar where to find food."
- *Appeal for help.* "Cleanse me...wash me. Create in me a pure heart, O God," David cries. Then he adds, "Grant me a willing spirit, to sustain me." That is like saying, "Make me willing to

be willing, Lord, and keep on doing so." That is not a bad prayer for one who wants an effective outreach.

- *Abdication of supposed "throne rights."* I use the word "supposed" because Christians don't have the wherewithal to bring someone into God's kingdom anyway, but some Christians act as if they do. They approach witnessing as if it all depends on them. It is their job to "save the lost." Oh, if they only could! Oh, if *we* only could! Unfortunately, it takes a few losing arguments with someone we are trying to "save" to show us how powerless we are.

It is "God who saves," David reminds us (v. 14). He is the One who has the ability to break down barriers, cut through religiosity and soften hard hearts. The only One. The whole salvation process is His, and each Person in the Trinity is involved. A Scotsman is said to have described God's plan of redemption this way (catch the marvelous accent!):

> The Father thought it
> The Son bought it
> The Spirit wrought it
> But I've got it.

Others can have it, too, but for that to happen, we must...

JUMP INTO THE SPIRIT'S FLOW

As the Spirit transports us to people in need, we are given the ability to listen with God's ears and to respond with God's wisdom. What will such a conversation sound like? Like Jesus Himself presenting the gospel! He had a way, you remember, of meeting people where they were. He spoke to a ruler about riches, to a Pharisee about birthrights and to a thirsty woman about water. He tailored each discussion to whatever was on the individual's heart. He let people know He cared. We can do likewise.

Having the Spirit of Christ living in us, we, too, can minister with sensitivity. We, too, can show love that draws people even when they are resisting. We, too, have the power of God's Word to accomplish what God desires.[9]

So, reader, for what are you waiting? As you are processing this information, do you have a yearning in your heart to break free from whatever it is that is keeping you from being a good witness for your Lord? Why don't you do it? Why don't you turn your outreach over to God's Spirit and let Him do your witnessing for you? Experience the relief that comes from transferring responsibility. Participate in the joy of watching other "beggars" find "food."

"Up to the waist," your guide keeps repeating.

You press your legs forward, making inroads in the water. Before long, you are half immersed. Not much farther to go.

I've done it! You think. *Now, which area will we be concentrating on next?*

Notes

1. See Exodus 12:11 *(KJV).*
2. Psalm 51:15.
3. Charles Haddon Spurgeon, *The Soul Winner* (Grand Rapids: Wm. B. Eerdmans Publishing Company, 1963), p. 31.
4. J. I. Packer, *Knowing God* (Downers Grove, Ill.: InterVarsity Press, 1973), pp. 34, 35.
5. Acts 1:5,8.
6. See Acts 4:31.
7. First Corinthians 3:6.
8. Mark 16:15.
9. See Isaiah 55:11.

Enveloping the Heart
(Our Hidden Desires)

~~~~~~~~

As water reflects a face,
so a man's heart reflects the man.

PROVERBS 27:19

You are up to your waist in water. You realize your chest will be immersed next—that area that envelops the heart, affecting your innermost passions and desires—those things you try to keep hidden from others.

As your guide invites you to let your heart come under the Spirit's control, you find yourself resisting. You are not alone.

Let me share with you a time when I too resisted—and needed help.

We were living in Michigan at the time. We were happy with our home, with our church and with the university our two youngest sons were attending. Suddenly our world was jarred. My husband, Lee, was offered a position in his company's home office. That meant a move to

New Jersey. (This is a move after the one described earlier.)

"Time to switch to a condo," Lee announced. "The twins are almost out of school, so we don't need a lot of room anymore. Besides, it would be nice not to have to cut the lawn and shovel snow."

At this stage in our lives a condo did make sense. To me, however, the word "condo" meant "townhouse." I was picturing a cute little ground-entry unit I could make cozy and warm. So I was totally unprepared for Lee's phone call from the East Coast.

"I've found the perfect 'condo,'" he informed me. "It's in a high-rise...14 stories up...right on the Atlantic Ocean." His voice was rising in intensity with every phrase. "The view is absolutely gorgeous! On a clear day you can see Manhattan!"

Now, you don't take a farm girl like me, plunk her down in a "hotel" and expect her to feel at home. My heart started to race. I was afraid I was going to have an attack—a big one!

Lee must have sensed my anxiety, for he added, "Just in case you don't want to live in a high-rise, I've also found a townhouse. I'll bring you the floor plans of both units. Then you can fly out and we'll examine them together. The final decision will be yours."

"Mine?" I asked in disbelief. Then I realized, *He means it! This husband of mine is willing to sacrifice his own desires in order to make me happy! But it wouldn't be right to take advantage of Him. However...*

As we pored over the two floor plans, I could feel my heart leading me to the townhouse. How cute it was! Larger than the high-rise unit, it had nooks and crannies that were begging for a creative touch. I could hardly wait to get at it! The unit also had a fireplace. I had to admit, though, that it had no view, and I knew the townhouse wasn't Lee's first choice.

What to do? Time for prayer, I decided. "Heavenly Father," I began, "in all the years Lee and I have been together, there have been very few times when we have disagreed over something major. I don't want this to be one of them. As I fly out to look at these two condos, make Lee and me of one mind." That prayer meant, of course, "Lord, change Lee's mind!"

Guess whose mind the Lord changed? When I saw the landscape from 14 floors up, I fell in love with the "condo" by the ocean. As you know from chapter 4, we ended up living there.

How do you explain what happened? I am not sure, except to say God took a farmer's daughter who had a "heart problem" and fixed it, giving her a heart compliant with her husband's desires and with His as well.

When I think about it, the problem I had was not unique. "Heart trouble" seems to be...

A UNIVERSAL DISEASE

We all experience irregularities in our emotions, our motives, our intentions and our desires—those things that have their beginnings in our hearts. We dismiss our discomfort as "normal," though, and get on with our lives.

The day comes, however, when we can no longer ignore our symptoms. They are too serious. We are developing tendencies to deceive, to disobey, to betray, to get even and to do many more unhealthy things. In the past we have relied on favorite home remedies such as rationalization and self-justification, but they are not working the way they used to. We need something more lasting; and we need it immediately.

For those who have experienced a spiritual new birth, confession of daily sins keeps their new hearts pure. For those who may not be sure they have been "born again," however, the problem is more serious. Although they may have learned to "walk" as Christians do, to pray as Christians are supposed to and even to share their faith with a lost world, inside they wonder if they have ever had a real spiritual conversion themselves.

In the providence of God, there is hope. Every seeker has a mentor. For you, the reader, there is your faithful guide. He senses any uncertainty you might have. He wants to make sure you have a personal relationship with God through the Lord Jesus Christ, and he wants to make sure that you know you have it.

"Up to your shoulders," your mentor is saying. "Let God's Spirit cover your chest. Then, and only then, will you experience a heart change that is permanent." You need to become...

A Heart Patient
You are nervous. You don't like doctors. You are a private person and to you doctors are "invasive." Here you are in a doctor's waiting room, though, filled with uncertainties. *Will the Doctor be able to cure me? How much will His services cost? Will I be able to pay?*

At the moment, your pain has subsided. You are glad your guide has decided to come with you. As you are waiting to be called, you can't help eavesdropping on a conversation that is being carried on between two patients seated near you.

"I wouldn't be here without the Doctor," one testifies. "I owe my life to Him."

"Me too," the other chimes in. "He's a Miracle Worker. You should have seen me this time last year. Could hardly make it from the car. But look at me now," he says, as he stands up and dances a jig, arms in the air. "I'm a new person."

Everybody in the room claps. You clap, too, but your eyes have shifted elsewhere—to a table next to your chair. On top is a black leather Book and next to it a stack of white papers. TAKE ONE, a sign invites. You do. *Perhaps this is meant to reassure the patients*, you hope as your eyes fly over the words:

> Welcome to the office of the Great Physician. Don't let your heart be troubled. You have come to the right place—to a Cardiologist of world renown. He has practiced His specialty in every corner of the globe, even living among some of His patients in order to "feel their pain." In His travels He has made quite a Name for Himself, not only for His compassion, but also for His expertise. You see, He cures all who come to Him. Furthermore, He does so without cost to His patients. If you wish to read about some diagnoses and cures, consult one of the black leather Books scattered throughout the office.
> —*The Office Staff*

You take the advice. You pick up a Book near you and begin to leaf through its pages. Your eyes fall on the following words:

> "There is no one righteous, not even one; there is no one who understands, no one who seeks God. All have turned away, they have together become worthless; there is no one who does good, not even one. Their throats are open graves; their tongues practice deceit. The poison of vipers is on their lips. Their mouths are full of cursing and bitterness. Their feet are swift to shed blood; ruin and misery mark their ways, and the way of peace they do not know. There is no fear of God before their eyes."[1]

A strange diagnosis for a cardiac patient, you muse. *It mentions throats, tongues, lips, mouths, feet and eyes—but not the heart.* Before you have time to read further, however, the door to the Doctor's inner rooms opens and there He is: the Great Physician Himself!

His appearance takes your breath away. *Is He of this world or of another?* you wonder. *Either I'm having a celestial vision, or I've been transported to heaven!* Whichever, you recall the description the apostle John gave when He "saw the Lord": "His head and hair [are] white like wool," John said, "and his eyes [are] like blazing fire. His feet [are] like bronze glowing in a furnace, and his voice [is] like the sound of rushing waters."[2]

"Welcome," the Doctor says, His syllables rumbling off the walls of the room. As He speaks, you are mentally transported back to the time you imagined you were Moses climbing that shaky mountain to receive the Ten Commandments. Now you are in the presence of the same One Moses encountered. You fall to your knees.

"He didn't come to frighten us," you remember Charles Swindoll saying in *The Finishing Touch,* "but to show us the way to warmth and safety."[3] It is true. You notice compassion in His face, and love. You also notice a gentleness in the way He is extending His hand. You rise.

"Follow me," He says.

You do. Right into His office. Your guide asks if he may come with you.

"Of course," the Great Physician answers. "I remember when you yourself first came to me. Thanks for bringing a friend this time." The door closes behind the three of you.

"I'm glad you came," the Doctor says to you, as He takes His seat behind the desk and motions to you to take yours. "Let's get right down to business. What brings you here?"

"Discomfort in the chest area, Doctor—discomfort that affects everything I do."

"Any history of heart problems in your family?"

"Yes. My father, my mother, my..."

"We'll take a picture of your heart in a moment to see how extensive the damage is. But first, I want to show you...

A Model of a Perfect Heart

"Look here. See how intricate the design is? This is the organ that determines whether or not the rest of the body remains healthy. The motives, the intentions and the desires of the whole person begin here, along with the emotions that go with them. The heart is responsible for what circulates to the other parts: to the mind, suggesting what it should dwell upon; to the eyes, influencing what they should watch and read; to the ears, affecting what they should listen to; to the mouth, monitoring how it should express itself; to the hands, urging them to do this or that; and to the feet, indicating the direction they should go. A diseased heart spreads disease. A healthy heart pulsates with purity, sending vitality to the whole body. 'Blessed are the pure in heart,' I like to remind my patients, 'for they will see God.'"

You feel weak. Your own heart is anything but pure. You remember the unrighteous people you read about in the black leather Book—people whose throats, tongues, lips, mouths, feet and eyes were diseased. You felt as if you yourself were being described. When you were reading, you never got to the part that pinpointed the cause of the dysfunction. Now you know what it is: a diseased heart.

"I need that X ray, Doctor," you blurt out. "And I need it now! Furthermore, I want You to interpret it for me. 'Search me, O God, and know my heart; test me and know my anxious thoughts. See if there is any offensive way in me, and lead me in the way everlasting.'"

"I will," He promises. "I search every heart and understand every motive....You see, patients like you come in here looking pretty good. Sometimes they're not even in pain. So when they see their X rays, they are shocked. Here at the clinic, we use a very accurate machine called 'The Word.' It has the ability to 'penetrate' the heart's deepest recesses and to 'judge' the intentions hidden there. Under its scrutiny 'everything is uncovered and laid bare.'[4] Are you ready for such a self-revelation?"

"As ready as I'll ever be."

"Good. When you leave this room, turn right. You will see 'X ray' down the hall. Your friend may go with you."

After the X Ray
You find yourself back in the Doctor's office. "It's a disturbing report," the Doctor says, placing the film on a view box. "Look at this picture. There's a destructive thought lurking in this chamber and a slanderous intent in that one. I see an adulterous desire here and a false witness there.[5] You can't live long like this."

"Doctor, there was a paper on the table in the waiting room that says You cure all who come to You."

"It's true. I do. You don't have to die. I can save you. But in order to do so, I must perform surgery. For the record, let me assure you I am certified to do the type you need. In fact, I am the only Physician who is. Because of My unique understanding of heart problems, many people come to Me, and I perform the same type of surgery on all of them."

"What type is it, Doctor?"

"A transplant. You need a heart transplant. A bypass won't work for you. That would be like putting a bandage on a cancer. You need to have your diseased heart removed and replaced with a healthy one. As I said, I'll do the transplant Myself. I want to make sure you get a heart like Mine. While I'm at it, I will put My Spirit in you and move you to follow My decrees and be careful to keep My laws."[6]

"You mean I'll have a whole new motivation?"

"Absolutely. You'll be new from the inside out."

"When can you schedule me?"

"The sooner the better. This is an emergency."

Things get a bit hazy after that. You do remember your guide praying with you and the kind eyes of your Physician peering over His mask. You also remember hearing, "It's out! The sin is out!" You recall wondering, *What will it be like having a new heart beating within me and a new Spirit influencing my decisions?* You soon find out.

What a Change!

You can hardly believe the difference. Your face begins to radiate with a new glow. You have a youthful zip to your walk. You have never felt better in your life! You wonder why it took you so long to admit you needed help.

You go for your first postoperative visit and wait for the results of a new X ray—the first after your surgery. Your friend is sitting beside you. The Doctor comes in.

"I'll give you the good news a little at a time," He begins with a twinkle in His eye. "As I mention each thing I see on the film, tell me if what I say is borne out in your experience."

"Okay."

"Your new X ray shows a heart that's pure."

"Correct. I really can't stand to watch, to read, or to be associated with 'garbage' anymore. It's gone from my life. Gone!"

"Good. But be careful. Old desires can creep back in very subtly. Hmm...I also see a heart that's loyal."

"Right. If I even think about betraying someone, I feel a twinge of guilt. My new heart is keeping me true."

"Again, be alert. New hearts become diseased, too. Now, how about peace? Do you experience peace?"

"Peace that transcends understanding.[7] Even in times of turmoil."

"I also see a heart that yearns for spiritual things."

"You know, doctor, it's amazing. I used to think daily Bible reading was only for spiritual giants. Now I'm in God's Word every day myself. I can't seem to get enough of it. I want to learn all I possibly can so that when I meet the Father face-to-face, we'll have lots to talk about."

The Doctor smiles. "I also see love. And forgiveness. And patience. And..."

"How about gratitude, Doctor? Is that on your film? It should be, because right now I feel so much of it I can't express it. I am over-whelmed that You would go to so much trouble for me!"

"You don't know the half of it," He responds, with a faraway look.

"How can I thank You?"

"In a couple of ways," the Doctor responds. "First of all, make regular appointments so that we can develop a deeper relationship. By the way, you won't have to come to my office. I am one Physician who still makes house calls.

"Also, make it known there is hope for the dying. Send Me some more patients, will you? Now, before you go, a word of advice: Keep that new heart in good working order. Eat right and get plenty of exercise. We especially recommend exercising in water."

"Water?" you ask incredulously. "You want me to exercise in water?"

Back to the River!

You are still standing in water up to your waist. "Up to the shoulders," your guide is repeating. "Give that brand-new heart of yours a workout."

"It's getting a workout all right," you say as you push your way forward. "The deeper I go, the harder it gets."

"That is true only up to a point. At some point it will get easier. You won't feel your own weight as much. Right now you are trying to progress in the efforts of the flesh. You're relying on self-improvement techniques. You don't need to get better at what you're doing. You need to give up—totally—and let the Spirit do the 'doing.'

"By the way, did you notice that the deeper you go, the less of Self is showing? Before long, Self won't be visible at all. People will look in your direction and see Christ. That's good, you know. Very good."

"I like what is happening!" you exclaim. "I can't wait to see what's coming next."

"When you find out, you may not be so enthused," your guide confirms.

Let's see if he is right.

Notes

1. Romans 3:10-18.
2. Revelation 1:14,15.
3. Reflections, quoted in *Christianity Today* (December 9, 1996): 50.
4. This section is based on the following Scripture verses: Matthew 5:8; Psalm 139:23,24; 1 Chronicles 28:9; Hebrews 4:12,13.
5. Taken from Matthew 15:19.
6. Based on Ezekiel 36:26,27.
7. Philippians 4:7.

II

Over the Head
(Our Control Center)? No!

Be made new in the attitude of your minds.
EPHESIANS 4:23

You have now advanced up to your neck. You can feel the water lapping at your chin. You are proud to have come this far, but you are scared. Very scared. It is hard to keep your feet on the ground. Let them rise, and you will drown. Panic strikes. "Enough!" your brain cries out. "This is far enough!"

It is easy to understand your fear. You have begun your new life with Jesus and you are not sure what lies ahead. Right? Well, one thing you can be certain of: Your Savior has a high goal for you. He wants to make you just like Him.

Having said that, let me ask you this: Do you remember how Jesus began His ministry? By being baptized in a river. He let the water cover His head. Do you see some role modeling here?

Admittedly, the head is the hardest part for you to submerge. For it represents your control center: that which decides what you think, watch, listen to and say—those things that identify you as being "you." In reality, however, the real "you" hasn't emerged yet, and it can't until you "take the plunge."

That is true for all of us. We can never become all God wants us to be until we let the Spirit cover our attitudes. We are meant to submit, not to control; to flow with the Spirit, not to fight against Him; to fit into a plan bigger than our own agendas—a plan that extends from eternity past into eternity future. Submit to this plan and the rewards are great. Refuse and God's blessings are bypassed, perhaps forever. So it is important to submerge those last few inches of the body.

CONSIDER A MIND BOGGLER

How important is your head to your identity? Or, to put it another way, how much of your body could be lopped off and you would still be "you"?

This was the question raised in a discussion group of which I was a member. I will not divulge who said what, but I will share the group's conclusions. First of all, everybody agreed that it is possible to lose fingers and toes, hands and feet, even arms and legs without losing your identity. They also agreed that if you gave up some parts that are internal, such as an appendix, a uterus or a section of your colon, you would still be your old recognizable self (phew!). They also concluded that organs or blood received from another person would not alter who you are. However, should you lose your head, that would be another story. Who could then identify you? The head is essential for recognizing who a person is.

Consider...

A SPIRITUAL PARALLEL

Jesus Christ is the "head of the church."[1] Our Christian identity lies in Him. As long as He is directing the course of our lives, and we are acting in accordance with His commands, it is easy for others to recognize us as Christians. Reject His control and replace it with our own, however, and the result is confusion. *Does this person belong to the Body of Christ or not? With Self in the place of prominence, how can he or she be a Christian?*

This is why we need a total immersion in the Spirit of Christ. Our heads have to "disappear" and be covered by the "water."

"Isn't this book, then, written backward?" you may say. "Shouldn't it start with the head instead of with the feet?"

Perhaps it should. It might—if living the Christian life were a simple discipline, but it is not. "Immersion in God's Spirit" can be an extremely complex experience, even occurring "backward" at times. What happens

> In the process of opening our ears, the Spirit will teach us how to detect His "still, small voice"— a voice that can easily get drowned out in the cacophony of sounds that dominate everyday life.

in practice does not always fit our intentions. For example, when presented with the claims of Christ, we say, "I want to submit all that I am to all that God wants me to be." Sounds great, but when it comes to "working out" this commitment, we resist "taking the plunge." Instead, we settle for a gradual yielding to the Spirit's control. Rarely does it start with the head.

Just think about the struggle that comes as each tiny part of the head is submerged. Consider...

THE EARS

If you are like me, you will be more apt to tilt your head backward instead of forward, letting the water cover your ears before it reaches your face. That is not necessarily bad, for the ears are very important. Even little children in Sunday School know that. "Be careful, little ears, what you hear," they sing. They are learning that what they listen to determines, in part at least, what they will eventually become.

Try turning your listening habits over to the Spirit. Let Him plug and unplug your ears. For example, let Him close them to that which is harmful—to words that are degrading, inciteful, slanderous or blasphemous—in music as well as in the spoken word. Let Him open them to that which is beneficial. Granted, sometimes we may have to be hurt to benefit from someone's counsel, but in the end we will realize that the words spoken were for our own good.

In the process of opening our ears, the Spirit will teach us how to detect His "still, small voice"—a voice that can easily get drowned out in the cacophony of sounds that dominate everyday life—sounds that come from clocks, bells, whistles, horns, motors, engines, faxes, copiers, computers, radios, TVs, CDs and people. The apostle John says, "He who belongs to God hears what God says."[2] What an encouragement to open the Bible for the express purpose of listening to what the Spirit might be saying! When we do that, we are making it clear that we will not let His voice be drowned out.

When duties become overwhelming, however, it can be difficult to hear the Spirit's voice. Andrew Murray cautions, "There is a restlessness and worry that come of care and anxiety about earthly things; these eat away the life of trust and keep the soul like a troubled sea. There the gentle whispers of the Holy Comforter cannot be heard."[3] That is when it becomes oh-so-important to lie back in the "water" and let it lap over your "ears." Then, and only then, is it possible to tune out what may be detrimental to Christian growth and tune in to what is essential.

Now, on to...

THE MOUTH

This is a troublesome part of the body—the part that, according to the Bible, "no man can tame." Once the Spirit covers our tongues, though, some exciting things begin to happen. For starters, we are given new freedom to praise the Lord. In the words of the Bible, the Spirit puts "a new song in [our] mouth, a hymn of praise to our God."

We are also given a holy boldness in presenting the gospel. We may even become like the apostle Peter, who, after being warned to stop preaching about Jesus, exclaimed, "We cannot help speaking about what we have seen and heard."

As a result of this boldness, we may find ourselves in some pretty tough situations, but the right words will come. The Bible says, "'Do not worry beforehand about what to say. Just say whatever is given you at the time, for it is not you speaking, but the Holy Spirit.'" Talk about being "covered"! This is one time we can be very thankful that we are!

The Spirit knows when to embolden and when to restrain—something that is pretty hard to judge for ourselves. How many times have you said something you wish you could take back? Unbridled outbursts "grieve the Holy Spirit of God," the apostle Paul says. Then he adds, "Do not let any unwholesome talk come out of your mouths, but only what is helpful for building others up."

This is a difficult discipline if attempted on our own, but with the Spirit's help, compliance becomes effortless. He wants to do our speaking for us. The listener, then, receives a blessing, and we are left wondering, *Did those uplifting words come from ME?*

Yes, they did. "O, Lord," the psalmist exclaimed, "how sweet are your words to my taste, sweeter than honey to my mouth!"[4] Don't you love it? Now let's talk about...

THE EYES

The Bible contains some wonderful accounts of people whose eyes were "immersed."

Saul's Dramatic Experience

Remember Saul, the Pharisee whose goal was to see all Christians annihilated? He dedicated his life to ferreting them out and watching with satisfaction as they were imprisoned, tortured and stoned. He wasn't very careful about what his "little eyes" feasted on, was he?

We can never underestimate the power of the Spirit, however. As Saul was on his way to Damascus to persecute more Christians, God stopped him with a blinding light. As a result, he was sightless for three days. Then the Lord commissioned Ananias to meet with him. "The Lord— Jesus...sent me so that you may see again," Ananias informed Saul, "and be filled with the Holy Spirit."

Dr. Luke records, "Immediately, something like scales fell from Saul's eyes, and he could see again. He got up and was baptized." The result was a mighty change in Saul. Whereas before he viewed followers of Jesus Christ as a threat to his religion, later he saw them as brothers and sisters in the faith. It is amazing what a covering of the eyes can do!

Job's Transformation

Job is another example of a man whose spiritual eyesight was transformed. After enduring a series of incredible tragedies, he was drenched in a thunderstorm, you will remember. In the midst of that storm—the lightning flashing, thunder rolling and rain coming down in torrents—his eyes were touched by God. He sensed a change. As he looked heavenward, he exclaimed, "My ears had heard of you but now my eyes have seen you."

What did he see? He saw a Sovereign. He saw a God who could take something as heartbreaking as tragedy and turn it into something good. The experience was life changing.

The Blind Man's Faith

The Bible also tells of an unnamed man who was blind from birth. One day Jesus came his way, "spit on the ground, made some mud with the saliva, and put it on the man's eyes." Then Jesus told the man to wash off the mud in the pool of Siloam. The man did as he was told and was cured. When asked by some religious leaders how one sinner could heal another (they refused to believe Jesus was God), the man said he didn't know. "One thing I do know," he added. "I was blind but now I see." What a testimony!

Our Bigger Vision

We, too, will be able to make that statement, once we let the water cover our eyes. For the first time in life we will see things clearly. We will see ourselves for who we were: people in need of help. We will see God for who He is: an awesome Creator reaching down to His helpless creatures. We will also see the world for what it is: a bunch of frantically lost individuals who need to hear the good news that Someone cares. We will want to be the bearers of this good news. We will want to be like Saul, Job and the blind beggar—all rolled into one.

After the Spirit touches our eyes, we will not only become aware that we have a bigger vision, but we will become conscious of our "smaller" vision as well, of what we choose to look at in the routine of our everyday lives. "Turn my eyes away from worthless things," the psalmist prayed. "Open my eyes that I may see wonderful things in your law."[5] Oh, to saturate ourselves with these "wonderful things" to the point that they become part of us! Our Helper will see that they do.

Next, let's consider...

THE NOSE

The very thought of water in the nostrils brings on panic. *I'm going to die*, we think, and correctly so.

What, however, is so horrible about dying? To really live, my friend, you *must* die—die to your dreams, die to your plans, die to your schemes, die to the old "you." "There is a death to self in coming into the stream of the Spirit,"[6] Samuel Shoemaker confirms. It is something we should expect.

"Don't you know," the apostle Paul emphasizes, "that all of us who [are] baptized into Christ Jesus [are] baptized into his death? We [are] therefore buried with him through baptism into death in order that, just as Christ was raised from the dead...we too may live a new life." There it

> Jesus lets us become part of
> His experience so that He
> may become part of ours.

is: God's order of things. Not life, then death, as is commonly thought. But death, then life, as the Bible teaches. "If we [die] with him, we will also live with him,"[7] Paul tells Timothy.

The phrase "with him" suggests a two-way identification: an identification of the believer with Christ and an identification of Christ with the believer. Jesus lets us become part of His experience so that He may become part of ours. Therefore, the One whose own breath was cut off takes the hand of the hesitant bather and whispers, "Let it happen. Let death come."

Friend, I know this is a hard teaching, but that is why you have a guide. He is also a "swimming instructor." Learn to trust him, for he knows how to prepare his pupils for the difficult lessons ahead. He begins by teaching...

The Dead Man's Float
Under your swimming instructor's guidance you will learn how to put your face into the water, slide your arms forward so they are touching

your ears, and shove off, letting your body glide. You will learn to let the water support you. You will be calm. You will also be weightless. How good it will feel!

The darkness will gently cradle you, enveloping you more and more. It will seem as if you are in a big, black, peaceful void. You will be totally relaxed. *No wonder they call it the "dead man's float,"* you will think as you drift into nothingness.

Then out of the void you will hear a voice: "Good job!"

You will awaken from your reverie with a start. Your brain will become alert, signaling your head to pop out of the water and your feet to seek the sandy bottom. You will stand. You will gulp in great quantities of air. Then you will open your eyes, move your fingers, stretch your legs and try out your voice. *They work! I must be alive!* you will think. *I have survived putting my head into the water and floating facedown. Now I'm ready to learn how to swim.*

That is how it will be, my friend, but you are not there yet, are you? You haven't put your head under yet. Something is holding you back. Let me guess what it is. It is...

The Mind
We are talking now about your control center, that part of you that generates thoughts, forms words, dictates actions and shapes character. We are talking about destiny. Giving up control of your destiny is a great fear, isn't it? What if I told you your destiny was never yours to control anyway? Would it, then, be easier to "give up"?

I am guessing another fear involves your conscience, that part of you that distinguishes right from wrong. You are afraid the Holy Spirit may want access to that, too. In fact, He does. According to Charles Stanley, "The Holy Spirit uses the conscience as a primary avenue of communication."[8] Uh-oh! That means you will have to start listening to it. Do I detect some resistance here?

I am also guessing you are afraid that once the Holy Spirit takes over your "head," you will become "so heavenly minded you are no earthly good"; that you will go around saying things such as "The Spirit led me..." or "The Spirit told me...." Relax. The Spirit can and does lead and speak directly. His guidance comes through a great gift from God with which you are already very familiar: your conscience. The Spirit uses the Bible to keep that conscience on track.

You, however, are still responsible to use your mind: to read the Bible, to pray, to consider circumstances, to obtain counsel, to make advantage-disadvantage sheets, to know your personal inclinations and God-given abilities. So in a sense, your mind will still belong to you. The "you" you will be then is not the "you" you are now, however. Then again, the "you" you are now is not the "you" you used to be. You are being sanctified—little by little—molded into the image of Christ.

Once your mind becomes immersed in the Spirit, you will aspire to goals that are loftier, think about plans that are bigger, have a perspective on everyday life that is eternal, adopt a value system that is uncompromising and replace your desire to control things with a desire to be like the Savior. In other words, you will be the "you" you were meant to be all along.

So don't just stand there. Do something. If you can't bring yourself to stick your head into the water, why not call for help? "Save me, O God, for the waters have come up to my neck,"[9] the psalmist cried. It is not a bad plea. For as someone has said, "Faith can be born in a cry."

Now What?

You are standing in water up to your chin. You have heard the benefits of putting your head under, but you are still scared to do it. You realize the decision you are facing is major. Do you identify totally with your Savior by "surrendering all," or do you fight to keep control? The promised "new Self" sounds better than the old one, but to get it, you have to move out of your comfort zone. You are not sure you want to do that.

"A great deal of our doubt and hesitation," Shoemaker says, "is fundamentally fear of letting ourselves go."[10] How true!

Stanley adds, "Until we give up, we aren't really in a position to be helped....When we recognize we can't make it, we are like a drowning man surrendering to the aid of his rescuer."[11]

Okay, you find yourself saying. *Suppose I do decide I want to surrender all. Then what? How do I go about doing it? I need advice. Make it practical, please.*

Notes

1. Ephesians 5:23.
2. John 8:47.
3. Andrew Murray, *Abide in Christ* (Fort Washington, Pa.: Christian Literature Crusade, 1968), p. 107.
4. In this section, the following Scripture verses are cited: James 3:8; Psalm 40:3; Acts 4:20; Mark 13:11; Ephesians 4:29,30; Psalm 119:103.
5. In this section, the following Scripture verses are cited: Acts 9:17,18; Job 42:5; John 9:6,25; Psalm 119:37,18.
6. Samuel M. Shoemaker, *With the Holy Spirit and With Fire* (New York: HarperCollins, 1960), p. 43.
7. In this section, the following Scripture verses are cited: Romans 6:3,4; 2 Timothy 2:11.
8. Charles Stanley, *The Wonderful Spirit-Filled Life* (Nashville: Thomas Nelson Publishers, 1992), p. 190.
9. Psalm 69:1.
10. Shoemaker, *With the Holy Spirit and With Fire*, p. 39.
11. Stanley, *The Wonderful Spirit-Filled Life*, p. 49.

PART THREE:
Practical Issues

~~~~~~~~~

Whatever you have learned or received or heard
from me, or seen in me——put it into practice.
And the God of peace will be with you.

PHILIPPIANS 4:9

12

Surrender! What if I Can't?

For I have the desire to do what is good,
but I cannot carry it out.

ROMANS 7:18

You are still up to your chin in the water. Your teacher is urging you to go under. You are past "principles" and "admonitions" now. You are at the point of action, but you can't do what is required. You just can't submerge that head of yours! You are imagining what would happen if you try. You are sure your immersion would not be a quiet dead man's float, like the one described. No. Your feet would fly up. Your arms would thrash around. You would swallow bucketfuls of water. You would emerge gasping for air. In other words, you would make a fool of yourself. You are sure.

"How am I supposed to do something I can't?" you ask your mentor. "I'm not a swimmer, you know. To swim one has to be able to support oneself in water."

"True. But to support oneself in water," your instructor counters, "one has to be able to swim."

"What?" you gurgle as the water laps into your mouth. "Learning to swim, then, must be impossible."

Yet you know it is not impossible. People learn to swim every day. Stretch your thinking. Relate learning to swim to trusting God, and listen to some thoughts attributed to C. S. Lewis. To believe in God, he taught, one must have faith. Yet to have faith, one must believe in God. It seems like an impossible hurdle, he admitted, yet daily, people place their trust in their Creator. How does it happen? Through a prayer like one mentioned in the Gospel of Mark: "I do believe; help me overcome my unbelief!"[1]

The dilemma you find yourself in is difficult by design. "When God purposes to do something through you," say the authors of *Experiencing God*, "the assignment will have God-sized dimensions."[2] This one certainly does. You yourself can't "do it." If you could, your faith would be your gift to God. In fact, it is God's gift to you. He has to be the One to "do it."

SO WHAT'S THE HANG-UP?

Your refusal to give up is the hang-up. You know you are in a battle, and the conflict will not stop until someone surrenders. You also know that the "someone" will not be God. He never surrenders.

The thought of being dubbed a loser is intolerable to you. It is to me, too. Our whole lives we have heard, "Go for the gold! You can do it! You're a winner!" Well, in this case we are not winners, at least not at first. Nobody fights God and comes out on top. Nobody. There is only one Winner in spiritual battles, and it is the Lord Jesus Christ.

Furthermore, the loser does not fare too well, at least not in the beginning. In Old Testament times when two groups of people were in conflict and one side was obviously losing, it was the custom of the surrendering king to approach the winning sovereign, bow before him and bare his neck in submission. The victor, then, would place his boot on the neck of the vanquished and raise his sword in triumph. At that point the winner would face several options. More often than not, he would choose the harshest. Down came the sword, and off came the head.

It sounds awful, doesn't it? Surrender to God's Spirit, followed by death to Self, which is what we are really talking about (again), is not an exciting prospect. Yet it is absolutely necessary. For death to Self is followed by resurrection to a new life—a new life in the Spirit.

Knowing this, it is still hard to make that decision to go all the way with God. "We do not leap easily into this stream," Samuel Shoemaker commiserates, "like a swimmer on a hot day into a cooling stream of water."[3] Indeed not. In fact, we are more like a little boy who doesn't want to be bathed, dragging his heels as his mother pulls him toward the tub.

What it comes down to is obedience. Our Commander-in-Chief is shouting, "Surrender!"

We are screaming, "No! I want to fight to the bitter end." The battle is an inner one, and, I might add, a timeless one. Humans have been engaged in war with God for centuries.

Remember Naaman, the Syrian army commander who was guilty of insubordination to his Creator? He had contracted leprosy, you recall, a debilitating disease for which he was seeking a cure.

"'Go, wash yourself seven times in the Jordan,'" was the order from God's prophet.

Naaman replied, "'Are not...the rivers of Damascus, better than any of the waters of Israel? Couldn't I wash in them and be cleansed?'" Then he turned and "went off in a rage," the Bible says. Now you would think he would be grateful for a cure from any source. But no. *This Hebrew God is not going to tell me, a Syrian army commander, where to go to get cured,* he was probably thinking. *I give the orders around here, not Him!*

When you find yourself in a continually losing situation, however, you do consider surrendering. "He went," the Bible says, "and dipped himself in the Jordan seven times, as the man of God had told him, and his flesh was restored and became clean like that of a young boy."[4] It is amazing what obedience can do.

It is too bad not everyone chooses to receive the blessings of obeying God. "If only you had paid attention to my commands," the Lord laments in the book of Isaiah, "your peace would have been like a river, your righteousness like the waves of the sea."[5] His words are appropriate for the challenge at hand, aren't they? They promise peace—an end to the war within and continual cleansing of the stubborn streak in all of us. To get to the place where we are willing to surrender, though, we have to own up to our problems. The first one to face is...

SELFISM

According to the Bible, selfism is one of the sins God hates the most. He calls it "pride and arrogance."[6] It boils down to trying to do what only God can do. "'My people have committed two sins,'" He declares in the book of Jeremiah. "'They have forsaken me, the spring of living water, and have dug their own cisterns, broken cisterns that cannot hold water.'"[7]

"Trying" is an enemy of trusting. Friend, you are "trying." Face your problem for what it is, and understand its origins. You, like me, have been ingrained with a pull-yourself-up-by-the-bootstraps mentality. "Believe in yourself; you can make it happen," caring adults have drilled into us. "I did it my way," popular crooners have bragged. As a result, we have bought into their philosophies.

> We can find our worth only in [Jesus Christ]. Only when we run into His outstretched arms do we begin to appreciate how much He really loves us, how valuable we are.

Although a teaching that encourages someone to reach his or her potential has a positive thrust, it can backfire—and can do so in the lives of the very ones needing help. For example, in the one who fails, it can produce low self-esteem, plunging the victim into a pit of despair. In the one who succeeds, it can produce inflated self-worth, elevating the person to a pedestal from which he or she thinks anything is possible, without any help from anybody, thank you!

"Don't notice me!" pleads the first victim, as she cowers in a corner. "Do notice me!" boasts the second, as he lifts his arms in personal triumph. In both cases, the emphasis is on "me," and in both cases, the victims of this humanistic indoctrination have been taught to bypass the source of true self-worth: Jesus Christ, the Redeemer.

Yes, we can find our worth only in Him. Only when we run into His outstretched arms do we begin to appreciate how much He really loves us, how valuable we are. "He fashioned me," we discover, "with the goal of making me like Himself. I have failed to submit to His purpose. This is sin, but with His blood He chose to cleanse me. Then He sent His Spirit to keep the cleansing process going. How special I must be! How much I must be worth!"

As appreciative as we are of our salvation, though, some of us still have trouble totally submerging Self. We just can't seem to do it.

"Why must you wait until you can do it before you do it?"[8] asks Marguerite Reiss in her book *Holy Nudges*. In other words, we must stop philosophizing and take action, letting whatever is going to happen, happen.

Oswald Chambers advises, "Watch yourself when the Spirit of God is at work. He pushes you to the margins of your individuality, and you either have to say, 'I shan't' or to surrender, to break the husk of individuality and let the personal life emerge."[9] Yet for this new Self to emerge, you have to get past your fixation on the old Self.

Once that is accomplished, we can face our second problem:

FEAR

Oh the fears we have! Fear of the unknown. Fear of failure. Fear of letting go. Fear of looking stupid. Fear of harm. Fear of death. These fears translate into questions. We find ourselves wondering, *What will happen if I get in over my head? Will I flounder? Will I thrash around like a madman? Will I look ridiculous? Will I get hurt? Will I drown?*

Now for the good news. Being afraid can produce positive results. When life is going along smoothly and there is nothing to fear, we become complacent. Let troubles come, however, and we turn to God. He, then, having our ear, reassures us. "Do not fear," He whispers, "for I am with you; do not be dismayed, for I am your God. I will strengthen you and help you; I will uphold you with my righteous right hand."[10] A loose paraphrase of this last statement might read, "I will teach you to float by holding My right hand underneath you."

But can I trust God to keep me from sinking? we wonder.

"There is a single second when faith becomes stronger than fear,"[11] Marguerite Reiss answers. That moment belongs to God, not to us. We don't even need to know when it happens.

In *Hind's Feet on High Places*, Much Afraid, the allegorical character who is on a journey of faith to the "high places," learns the secret of

> As you face your fears and let God conquer them, you...will be able to obey that "glorious urge" to "give yourself with no reserve."

"the abandonment of self-giving" as she watches a thunderous waterfall fling itself over a ledge in an apparent suicide mission. To ease her terror, her Shepherd explains that appearances can be deceiving:

> At first sight perhaps the leap does look terrible...but as you can see, the water itself finds no terror in it....It has only one desire, to go down and down and give itself with no reserve or holding back of any kind. You can see that as it obeys that glorious urge, the obstacles which look so terrifying are perfectly harmless and indeed only add to the joy and glory of the movement.[12]

As you face your fears and let God conquer them, you, too, will be able to obey that "glorious urge" to "give yourself with no reserve." But first things first.

You must overcome a third problem:

LACK OF TRUST

You are worried that the water won't hold you up. Right? Read 2 Kings 6. If God can make an axhead float, He certainly can do the same for you.

John Powell, in *A Reason to Live! A Reason to Die!*, observes: "Most of us, in our desire for a meaningful faith seem to be saying to God, 'Show me and I'll believe'....The process must be reversed. He is saying to us, 'Believe in Me and I'll show you.'"[13]

Dietrich Bonhoeffer takes this reasoning a step further. To us who are thinking, "Once I believe, I'll obey," Bonhoeffer says, "Unless he obeys, a man cannot believe."[14] So we are back to the task of trying to separate faith from action.

It is an impossible assignment. The two are quite inseparable. Together they comprise the word "trust"—a combination that F. B. Meyer sums up this way: "God must have the entire trust of the soul....From the deep waters that overflow you, cry to God....He will stretch out His right hand and catch you, saying, 'O thou of little faith, wherefore didst thou doubt?'"[15]

If you have never owned up to your lack of trust before, these words should help you do it.

We are not finished yet, though. We need to consider at least one more problem, and that is...

THE STRENGTH OF THE HUMAN WILL

The human will simply does not want to submit to God's will. It is a fact of life that needs to be faced up front. Otherwise, once we are in the deep part of the river, we could find ourselves swimming against the current. That can be tiresome—and thoroughly frustrating. Once, however, we make a decision to go with the flow of God's Spirit, we find ourselves being carried effortlessly to wherever God wants us to be—and enjoying every bit of the ride.

Charles Stanley says, "As believers, our potential for righteous living is in direct proportion to our willingness to allow the Holy Spirit to produce His fruit through us."[16] The crux of the matter lies in the word "willingness," doesn't it?

Listen to Rees Howells, the Welsh missionary, tell how the Holy Spirit "spoke" to him about his admitted unwillingness to submit, the struggle that ensued and the difference it made when he gave in to the Spirit's overtures. The Holy Spirit begins the conversation:

> "Are you willing?"
> "How can self be willing to give up self?..."
> "If you can't be willing, would you like Me to help you? Are you willing to be made willing?..."
> I bowed my head and said, "Lord, I am willing."
> Immediately I was transported into another realm, within the sacred veil, where the Father, the Savior, and the Holy Ghost live. There I heard God speaking to me, and I have lived there ever since.[17]

Just think, this exciting transformation was the result of mere submission to the Holy Spirit of God! Yet that submission is never easy.

Jesus, however, recognizes our struggle. To the Jews who were persecuting Him, He said, "'These are the Scriptures that testify about me, yet you refuse to come to me to have life.'" Then again, "'How often I have longed to gather your children together, as a hen gathers her chicks under her wings, but you were not willing.'"

Jesus recognizes this struggle in others because He had a battle with His own will. "'Take this cup from me,'" He pleaded as He faced the pain of the cross. But He was careful to add, "'Yet not my will, but yours be done.'" With the word "yet" release came, and He could continue to live out His stated purpose for coming to earth: "'I have come to do your will, O God.'"[18]

The good news is that because Jesus identifies with our struggles we can identify with His victory. His triumph can become our triumph, but we must let it. The "letting" begins with facing our shortcomings, then preparing for a dramatic change. Marguerite Reiss tells us to get ready for a jolt:

> It is a shock to jump when you've never walked;
> To walk when you're used to crawling;
> To crawl when you're used to lying down.
> Remember the man by the pool?
> His words to Christ were not
> "Oh, Lord, put me in the water." But—
> "Lord, I cannot."[19]

He admitted his weakness to God. Then came the miracle.

OKAY, NOW WHAT?

"I admit my own shortcomings," you say to your mentor. "I am hampered by pride, overwhelmed with fear, unable to trust and engaged in a battle of the wills—a battle I can never win. Actually, I don't want to win. I want to learn how to swim, but who's going to push my head under? Who will help me disappear in the water?"

Notes

1. Mark 9:24.
2. Henry T. Blackaby and Claude V. King, *Experiencing God* (Nashville: Broadman and Holman Publishers, 1994), p. 170.
3. Samuel M. Shoemaker, *With the Holy Spirit and With Fire* (New York: HarperCollins, 1960), p. 42.
4. Second Kings 5:10-14.
5. Isaiah 48:18.
6. Proverbs 8:13.
7. Jeremiah 2:13.
8. Marguerite Reiss, *Holy Nudges* (Plainfield, N.J.: Logos International, 1976), p. 139.
9. Oswald Chambers, *My Utmost for His Highest* (New York: Dodd, Mead, and Company, 1935), p. 346.
10. Isaiah 41:10.
11. Reiss, *Holy Nudges*, p. 120.
12. Hannah Hurnard, *Hind's Feet on High Places* (Grand Rapids: Fleming H. Revell Co., 1973), p. 162.
13. John Powell, S.J., *A Reason to Live! A Reason to Die!* (Niles, Ill.: Argus Communications, 1972), p. 137.
14. Dietrich Bonhoeffer, *The Cost of Discipleship* (Indianapolis: The Macmillan Company, 1963), p. 72.
15. F. B. Meyer, *Daily Meditations* (Dallas, Tex.: Word Books, 1979), April 8.
16. Charles Stanley, *The Wonderful Spirit-Filled Life* (Nashville: Thomas Nelson Publishers, 1992), p. 72.
17. Norman P. Grubb, *Rees Howells: Intercessor* (Fort Washington, Pa.: Christian Literature Crusade, 1952), pp. 40, 41.
18. In this section, the following Scripture verses are cited: John 5:39,40; Matthew 23:37; Luke 22:42; Hebrews 10:7.
19. Reiss, *Holy Nudges*, p. 21.

13

Where Do I Go for Help?

~~~~~~~~

God is our refuge and strength,
an ever-present help in trouble.
PSALM 46:1

The scene is the same. You are standing in water up to your chin. You are immobilized. Your guide, who is now standing by your side, says, "You're still trying to bring about your own spirituality, aren't you? You can't believe that all God has for you is already yours." Indeed that is your problem.

Let's let Andrew Murray address the problem. "Believe that the fullness of the Spirit is indeed your daily portion," he says. "Be sure to take time in prayer to dwell at the footstool of the throne of God and the Lamb, whence flows the river of the water of life. It is there, and only there, that you can be filled with the Spirit."[1]

Taking time to dwell "at the footstool of the throne of God"—what a necessity! The more we do it, the better. No appointment is necessary, you know.

Your mentor has gone back to the beach to get a cell phone for you, so you can call heaven right now. But when you do, please realize to Whom you are speaking. The Person on the other end of the line is your Creator. Because of that, He is thoroughly acquainted with you—with your character traits, your personality quirks, your bents, your fears, your strengths, your weaknesses and everything else about you. It is He who endowed you with these things.

Remember, too, that He is omnipresent. "Where can I go from your Spirit?" the psalmist asks. "If I go up to the heavens, you are there; if I make my bed in the depths, you are there. If I rise on the wings of the dawn, if I settle on the far side of the sea, even there your hand will guide me, your right hand will hold me fast."[2] So in His Spirit God is with us "down here" while we are speaking to Him "up there." How comforting!

He is also all powerful, capable of meeting your every need. When you do come to the point where you surrender yourself to the "water," you will be relinquishing control to His Spirit, experiencing His Spirit's "fullness" in every aspect of your life. So keep in mind that you are speaking to the One who will be in charge of your future.

As you dial heaven, also remember you are consulting a trustworthy Constant in the ever-modulating flow of life. He is "the same yesterday and today and forever."[3] He never vacillates. He doesn't say one thing and do another. Nor does He make a decision on Monday and change His mind on Tuesday. There is no "Plan B" with God. "Plan A" is always in progress—even when it doesn't appear to be. I think you will really enjoy...

THE PHONE CALL TO
YOUR HEAVENLY FATHER

"T-H-R-O-N-E-R-O-O-M. Hello? Yes? To whom am I speaking please?"

"I AM WHO I AM."

"Sovereign Lord, I didn't realize I would be getting You directly. It's me, Your problem child. Let me introduce myself so You can know me better."

"Before I formed you in the womb I knew you. You are my offspring. You live and move and have your being in Me."

"Forgive me, Sovereign Lord. I didn't realize the extent of Your involvement in my life. Now You've got me curious. Do You know my present situation?"

"I am familiar with all your ways."

"Do You know what I'm thinking about?"

"I perceive your thoughts afar off."

"Do You know what I am about to say to You?"

"Before a word is on your tongue, I know it completely."

"You know, then, that there are areas in which I need reassurance. For example, I would like to hear You say You won't ever change Your mind about loving me."

"I the Lord do not change."

"I need to hear You say You will always have my best interest in mind."

"In all things I work for the good of those who love Me."

"I love You, Lord, with all my heart, but I have a strong will. I am worried that someday I may embark on a course that isn't right for me."

"In his heart a man plans his course, but I determine his steps."

"Really? How about my next step in this water? Will You be with me when I take it?"

"When you pass through the waters, I will be with you; and when you pass through the rivers, they will not sweep over you."

"What if I feel like I'm drowning?"

"When the righteous cry out, I hear them. I deliver them from all their troubles."

"What if my needs are too difficult for You?"

"Is anything too hard for the Lord?"

"In my mind I know nothing is, but my heart has questions. My immediate concern is a major one. I've been told I need Your Holy Spirit to come upon me in all of His fullness in order for me to experience all You have for me. My heart wants to know if this is possible."

"If you...know how to give good gifts to your children, how much more will your Father in heaven give the Holy Spirit to those who ask him!"

"Will You really do it, Sovereign Lord?"

"Be fully persuaded that I have power to do what I have promised."

"I just wish I could relax and let You move in my life. I wish I could let the 'water' support me, so to speak."

"The eternal God is your refuge, and underneath are the everlasting arms."[4]

"Underneath. Wow! That's the best place those arms could be. Thank You for the reassurance. I'll be calling again soon. Good-bye for now, Sovereign Lord." Click.

As you hand the phone back to your guide, you think about how all your life you have tried to do things yourself rather than letting God's Spirit take over. You bemoan...

THE PITFALLS OF BEING A SELF-HELP ENTHUSIAST

"I'd rather do it myself!"

"I can handle anything!"

"Fix the problem? What problem?"

We humans are a curious lot. Some people contact an expert at the slightest suggestion of trouble, while others, like those quoted earlier, try anything and everything before coming to the point of admitting their needs.

> We tend to fool around on our own a long time before turning to our expert Helper, God's Holy Spirit.

Unfortunately, their attitudes cause delays, and delays often make the problem worse. By the time help is summoned, the helper had better have good credentials, including lots of experience and ready availability, for these things will be needed.

"Why did you wait so long before calling me?" the expert is likely to ask. "Why did you try to fix it yourself?"

Couldn't the same two questions be asked of us Christians? Like our secular counterparts, we tend to fool around on our own a long time before turning to our expert Helper, God's Holy Spirit. Why the delay? Who knows? The Spirit has lots of experience assisting people in need and provides immediate service. Furthermore, He is the only One who can offer the help we need. He does make three requirements of us, however.

1. We must believe in Him.
2. We must receive the help He has to offer.
3. We must act on the reality of the promises He gives us.

Let's concentrate first on...

RECEIVING

Let me share a thought from Amy Carmichael. She has observed a natural phenomenon that has spiritual implications. It may help you. "The empty river-bed *inherits* the water that pours through it from the heights," she says, "it does not create the water, it only receives it, and its treasures are filled, its pools overflow for the blessing and refreshment of the land."[5]

Be like that empty riverbed, my friend. Don't try to "create" ways of going under the water. Don't even try to figure out how the Spirit might dunk you. Just be ready to receive whatever He has for you.

Now I admit that "inheriting water" is a strange concept, but therein lies its treasure. Let me explain.

Suppose you just found out you are about to inherit a small fortune. As you read and reread your attorney's letter, you become increasingly aware of the grace that is being bestowed upon you. You did not know an inheritance was being willed to you; but now that you have been informed, you can start acting on the truth of the promise. You had no hand in "creating" this windfall, but you are ready to receive it, for you know the desperate state of your finances.

Soon the promise will become reality. So each noon you run to the mailbox and rifle through the pile of letters. One day the anticipated gift is there. Immediately you spring into action. You pick up the envelope. You rip it open. You stare in amazement at the amount of the check. As soon as possible, you deposit that check. Then you know you can start making wise investments.

During this entire process you can't help marveling at what a blessing is yours. Your bank account, which was almost "empty," now overflows with "fullness." You didn't make it happen. Your benefactor did. But you received it. You didn't fight the blessing.

A similar condition exists when we receive Jesus Christ as our personal Lord and Savior. At that point we are adopted into the family of God and

> Some of us seem content to play
> in the shallows when we could
> be swimming in the depths.

come into our spiritual inheritance, which includes "every spiritual blessing in Christ,"[6] the Bible says. However, some of us live like spiritual paupers, nibbling on our peanut butter and jelly sandwiches when we could be dining with the King at a sumptuous banquet.

Look at this situation in the light of our water analogy. Some of us seem content to play in the shallows when we could be swimming in the depths. Swimming in the depths is where we belong. There we experience the Holy Spirit's "fullness." To receive it, though, we must act on the fact that this fullness is ours. We are talking now about...

APPROPRIATING THE SPIRIT'S RESOURCES

Just as our net worth goes from near zero to over-the-top when we invest a physical inheritance, so our spiritual net worth becomes full-to-

> Once a person is willing to die
> spiritually, it is much easier to die
> physically when the time comes.

overflowing whenever we invest our spiritual inheritance. How does it work? The Spirit's fullness becomes ours through an exchange. We exchange our "can'ts" for the Lord's "can's," our weaknesses for His strengths, our defeats for His victories, our brokenness for His wholeness and our death to Self for His resurrection to power.

This last exchange will bother you, I know, for you don't like the idea of dying. You don't even look forward to learning the dead man's float as part of your swimming instruction. It is wise, however, to get used to the concept of leaving one phase of life and moving on to the next. For there are many "deaths" in life. Whenever something comes up that we want to control, we have to "die" to that desire. The Spirit isn't able to move through us until we do. However, we are talking about spiritual death (a death to one's own agenda), not about physical death. I must say, though, that once a person is willing to die spiritually, it is much easier to die physically when the time comes.

> When we give Christ our inabilities, He replaces them with His supernatural strength.

In either case, death is the gateway to a better life. Spiritual death by "drowning," which is what everyone who submits to the Spirit's control undergoes, is an especially precious concept because it involves being enveloped by the Lord who loves us. "If we sink beneath the wave," F. B. Meyer says, "we will but fall into the hollow of God's hand, where the oceans are cradled."[7] In this "hollow of God's hand," there is rest for the soul that struggles.

Even physical death can be cushioned by the presence of God's Holy Spirit. Consider the Christian martyrs. Some sang, we are told, even as flames licked their flesh. Others asked God to bless their executioners as their heads were placed upon the block. How could they be so brave? They believed a better life was only seconds away. They reacted on the reality of that belief. They appropriated the promises of the future to the need of the present.

This appropriation takes place through the "exchange" I mentioned before. When we give Christ our inabilities, He replaces them with His supernatural strength. To understand this, try putting yourself...

IN A MARTYR'S SHOES

Imagine you are facing unbearable torture. You know that in your own strength you cannot go through it. So you cry out to God: "Jesus, help me. There is no way I can endure this pain."

"I know that," your Savior responds, "but I can. And I will. I will endure it for you. You see, I am qualified to help you. I have been where you are. I have felt what you are feeling. I have walked through the valley of death and have come out on the other side.

"The walk was not an easy one, but the Spirit went with Me all the way. In the Garden when I was sweating drops of blood, He was there. On the Cross, when My veins became 'swollen rivers of anguish' and My nerves 'strands of fire,' He was there. Even as My lungs filled with fluid, and I started to suffocate, He was right there with Me.

"He was the One who enabled Me to endure. For the joy that was set before Me, He empowered Me to persevere, causing Me to triumph, even over death.[8] He is prepared to do the same thing again, this time through you. Let Him. For whoever wants to save his life will lose it, but whoever loses his life for me will find it."[9]

The apostle Paul is a good example of someone who understood the significance of Jesus' words. Not only that, he appropriated them. "I have been crucified with Christ," he said, "and I no longer live, but Christ lives in me. The life I live in the body, I live by faith in the Son of God, who loved me and gave himself for me."[10]

By making these statements, Paul was doing more than verbalizing truths. He was claiming Christ's victory for himself. It is a victory that comes through a willingness to "die." Paul did die, not only spiritually, but physically as well. The first "death" made the second easier. Because the first was the result of obedience, the second became a privilege.

My friend, your loving heavenly Father has willed to you the same limitless resources He willed to the apostle Paul. They are flowing toward you from His throne in the form of promises. Open your heart to receive them. Reach out and embrace them. Make them your own through meditation, memorization and repetition. Keep on doing so until you have assimilated them—until you find yourself acting upon them. The promises of the Spirit's resources are not the same as the experience of receiving them, of course, but the promises prepare us for the reality of the experience when it comes.

Let me help you get started appropriating promises by selecting

Scripture verses that fit the occasion. Here they are: Psalm 46:1-4. Internalize them:

> God is our refuge and strength, an ever-present help in trouble. Therefore we will not fear, though the earth give way and the mountains fall into the heart of the sea, though the waters roar and foam and the mountains quake with their surging. There is a river whose streams make glad the city of God.

These are the words of our Lord. Reassuring, aren't they?

Through these Scripture verses and others we can redirect our vision and remind ourselves afresh where to turn for help: to the One who created us, knows us and went through hell to save us. He is now standing before us in the "water," offering His hand.

The question is, will we take the hand that is offered?

Will you? Will you let your Savior lead you into a deeper relationship with His Spirit?

"I want to," you reply. "Oh, how I want to. But will I?"

Notes

1. Andrew Murray, *Abide in Christ* (Fort Washington, Pa.: Christian Literature Crusade, 1968), p. 102.
2. Psalm 139:7-10.
3. Hebrews 13:8.
4. In this section, the following Scripture verses are cited: Exodus 3:14; Jeremiah 1:5; Acts 17:28; Psalm 139:1-4; Malachi 3:6; Romans 8:28; Proverbs 16:9; Joshua 1:5; Isaiah 43:2; Psalm 34:17; Genesis 18:14; Luke 11:13; Romans 4:21; Deuteronomy 33:27.
5. Amy Carmichael, *If* (Grand Rapids: Zondervan Publishing House, 1965), end of Section 6.
6. Ephesians 1:3.
7. F. B. Meyer, *Daily Meditations* (Dallas, Tex.: Word Books, 1979), May 13.
8. See Hebrews 12:2.
9. Matthew 16:25.
10. Galatians 2:20.

Here Goes!
I'm Taking the Plunge

"And if I perish, I perish."
ESTHER 4:16

You are still in water up to your chin. You are tense. You feel drawn to the safety of the beach, yet you don't want to miss the excitement of the river.

"I want to be where the action is," you say to your guide. "But to get there I have to submerge my head."

"Correct," he affirms.

"If I do, I might die."

"I doubt it," he counters, "but, of course, there's always that possibility."

"I know you've told me that being ready to die will make me ready to live, and I believe it. You've also told me that dying is better than living without full surrender to God's will. I believe that, too, but my beliefs have brought me to a crisis point. To plunge in or not to plunge in, that is the question."

"It is a question of obedience," your mentor answers.

Indeed it is a matter of obedience. Although our Commanding General's instructions are often called an "invitation," they do not include an RSVP. We are expected to comply. We can be comforted, though, that we have teachers to help us. They are prepared to lead us all the way—and to do so step-by-step.

They make it easy. Six steps are involved, each beginning with the letter *P*.

We can follow these steps whenever necessary. As was mentioned earlier, we have the option of stepping out of the water whenever we want to. Although we can never escape the Spirit's influence, we have the freedom to duck out from under His direct control. When we decide to come back, however, the process will always involve the same six steps. Step number one:

POSITION YOURSELF

God's desire, according to Blackaby and King, is "to get us from where we are to where He is working. When God reveals to you where He is working, that becomes His invitation to join Him. When God reveals His work to you, that is His timing for you to respond."[1]

Unfortunately, we become hung up on the possibility that another stream may exist somewhere—a stream that is less conspicuous and easier to enter. To address this concern, let me share a conversation from C. S. Lewis's work *The Silver Chair*. In this allegory, Aslan the Lion represents the Savior, and the character Jill is somebody just like us:

> "Are you thirsty?" said the Lion.
> "I am dying of thirst," said Jill.
> "Then drink," said the Lion.
> "May I—could I—would you mind going away
>   while I do?" said Jill.
> The Lion answered this only by a look and a
>   very low growl...
> "I daren't come and drink," said Jill.
> "Then you will die of thirst," said the Lion.
> "Oh, dear," said Jill, coming another step nearer.
> "I suppose I must go and look for another
>   stream then."

"There is no other stream," said the Lion.[2]

You see, my friend, this stream is *the* stream. It represents the work of God throughout the world. It refreshes the thirsty and revives the weary everywhere. It purifies sinners and brings hope to the despairing everywhere. It is the Spirit of the Sovereign Lord actively manifesting His redeeming power everywhere. At the point at which the stream passes by you, you have the opportunity of joining it. If you don't step into the water, it will continue to move on—and to do so without you.

You may not be sure you have enough faith to enter the river. However, "You don't need faith so much as a willingness to get in a position of belief,"[3] Marguerite Reiss points out. If you are positioned properly, the Lord will give you the faith to proceed.

You are promised an exciting future, not unlike what the Israelites anticipated when Moses affirmed, "For the Lord your God is bringing you into a good land—a land with streams and pools of water, with springs flowing in the valleys and hills."[4] If you turn back now, you may miss the greatest blessing of your life.

Andrew Murray said, "There is no safety except in advance. To stand still is to go back. To cease effort is to lose ground. To slacken the pace before the goal is reached is to lose the race."[5] So on to step number two:

PRESENT YOURSELF

"Offer your bodies as living sacrifices," the Bible says, "this is your spiritual act of worship."[6]

Now I know that sacrifices hurt. That is their nature. In this case, however, the sacrifices required are "living," so it doesn't "kill" us to make them. What God wants is a daily presentation of our faculties—a presentation similar to the one Jesus made when He said to the Father, "A body you prepared for me;...'Here I am—...I have come to do your will, O God.'"[7]

If this seems like a difficult assignment, it may help to remember that the same Spirit who prompted Jesus is now living in us. He has the same desire to say to the Father, "Here I am!"

It is up to us to appropriate the Spirit's willingness, to say, "Here is my body, Lord. I offer it up as a living sacrifice. Take my legs and move them forward. Take my heart and slow its anxious beat. Take my arms and enable me to reach out for assistance. And take my thoughts and focus them solely on You." Do you understand so far?

Now for step number three:

PROCEED FORWARD

The Christian life is designed to be an advance. It is a walk deeper into the Spirit, always deeper. The "immersion" that results is meant to be so

> The Christian life is designed to be an advance. It is a walk deeper into the Spirit, always deeper.

refreshing that we never again, not even for a moment, settle for a faith that is shallow. We are to love the depths of God's truth so much that the beach, offering its temptation to lie down and dry out, is only that—a temptation. We have decided to live our lives "dripping wet."

Proceeding forward in the Christian life, however, does involve risk. We talked about that earlier. We must be willing to leave our comfort zones; but knowing the Spirit is walking with us does indeed settle us.

It also brings an air of expectancy, for miracles accompany those who obey the Lord's commands. Take the experience of the Israelites as they positioned themselves by the river Jordan. They remembered their order. "'When you reach the edge of the Jordan's waters, go and stand in the river,'" Joshua had said. The people obeyed, and the Bible records a miraculous result: "As soon as...their feet touched the water's edge, the water from upstream stopped flowing. It piled up in a heap....So the people crossed over...on dry ground."[8]

Now I know the water doesn't part for everybody. The Spirit's plan for each of us is unique, but His intervention at our time of need can be just as spectacular. Now for the fourth step:

PRAISE GOD AS YOU GO

We need to get our focus off our own concerns. When the apostle Peter tried to walk on water, he concentrated on what the wind and the waves could do to him. The result was that he started to sink. If he had kept his gaze on the Lord, he would have reached his goal without any hassle. In a similar way, praise shifts our attention to the right Person and helps us to proceed without hindrance.

So, friend, forget about the dangers ("What will happen next?"). Or the consequences ("What will people think?"). Or the future ("Where will this step lead?"). Think only of God (who He is and what He is capable of doing). Think "now" (not next year, next month, next week, tomorrow or even the next minute). Seize the present moment and relish it.

> "There comes the place, the moment when we must launch out, make the plunge, put a leap into it and dare."

It takes only an instant for fear to be replaced by faith. That faith, of which you feel you have so little, will grow stronger moment by moment as you focus on the support those "everlasting arms" are giving you.

Well, that is it, my friend. I have told you all you need to know. Now is the time to...

PLUNGE IN

J. S. Bunting says, "There comes the place, the moment when we must launch out, make the plunge, put a leap into it and dare."[9]

Do I sense a discomfort with the "leap" part? Does it make the sanctification process, and its decision to go deeper into the Spirit, sound like something too easy to do? Listen to what C. S. Lewis has to say. He is reported to have posed this question: "Is it easy to love God?" Then he gave his own answer: "It is easy for those who do it."

So we ask ourselves, is it easy to commit to Someone who just awhile ago was almost a Stranger? Is it easy to lean back onto something that feels as though it won't hold you up? Is it easy to rest in arms you cannot see? Is it easy to surrender so-called "rights"? Is it easy to yield control? Is it easy to abandon the comfortable for the uncomfortable? Is it easy to trust that the bad will eventually turn out for good? Is it easy to wait for rescue? Is it easy?

The verbs *commit, lean, rest, surrender, yield, abandon, trust* and *wait* all require us to do something. Then when we have done it, God takes over. For example, leaning requires us to move before we can "let go." Yielding necessitates a calculated merging with the action going on around us before we get into the flow ourselves. Waiting demands a conscious effort to be still before whatever is going to happen can happen.

Being given these actively passive commands is like being told to go to sleep. How do you do it? The harder you work at it, the more elusive sleep becomes. We can do some helpful things, the experts tell us, such as tell our muscles, one by one, to relax, then concentrate until they do. The "letting go," however, occurs much sooner if we shift our focus from ourselves to the bed. How comfortable it will be! What relief it will bring to our tired bodies! How skillfully it will knit up our "ravell'd sleeve of care," as Shakespeare called it. Once our focus shifts from "trying" to trusting, the only thing we have to "do" is to lie back upon the bed. Then our heavenly Father takes over. Is it easy?

It is easy for those who do it.

"Okay," you say. "I have decided. I will do it!"

Before you have a chance to change your mind, you pinch your nose, scrunch your eyelids and go under. Immediately your feet shoot up, your arms thrash around and you swallow tons of water. Everything you feared is happening. Only for a moment, though. You remember what your guide told you to do. *Focus on the water*, you tell yourself. *Think of it as a Friend.*

The strategy works. You stop fighting. You allow yourself to be still. You feel the water beginning to lift you up. Out pops your head. You gulp for air. Your guide is right beside you, slipping his hand under your back, nudging you into a floating position. You let him. You start to relax. Then you feel your instructor beginning to remove his comforting support.

Don't panic, you tell yourself. *Underneath are my Father's everlasting arms. They will never be taken away.*

Floating in the river is about to treat you to some marvelous sensations. You open your eyes and look up. *Amazing! The sky is brighter than I have ever seen it!* you think. *The trees are greener; the flowers, more vibrant; the fruit, more luscious looking!* You feel as if a new creation has occurred, and you are right in the midst of it. The firmament is above you, natural wonders all around you, and the water underneath you. It is almost like being in heaven.

Suddenly, you are jolted back to reality. *I have swallowed too much of this water,* you think. Then you remember that a two-way "mystical union" is supposed to take place between the believer and the Holy Spirit of Christ.

"Well, I guess this is it," you say to the Lord, "I am in You, and You are certainly in me!"

As you lie there, you know, without being told, what the last step is going to be:

PAUSE TO REFLECT

So you reflect. You take time to enumerate those things that are no longer present in your life. Gone is your anxiety, tension and thrashing. Instead, you are experiencing peace, stillness and contentment. Maybe this is what Samuel Shoemaker was trying to communicate when he said, "We must let this stream of Grace do for us what we can never do by reason or effort."[10] Instead of "doing," you are "being" and "resting" and "letting." The relief is wonderful!

As you lie there floating, you concentrate on the feel of the water. You take time to savor the sensation it brings as it laps over and around your body. You focus on the gentleness with which it is caressing you. How soothing it feels as it ripples over your arms, your legs and your chest! You sense the cushioning strength of those "everlasting arms" beneath you, enveloping you in a loving embrace. Yes, your fear is gone, but a healthy respect for what the "water" can do is still there.

"Father God," you plead, "wash from my life all the dirt I have accumulated since I received a heart to know You. I want to be fresh and pure once again. I repent of my sins, my shortcomings and my failures. Resume control of my life."

After that confession you feel a "rush." It is as if the Lord is not only around you, but surging through you as well. You feel Him touch your heart. It is skipping a beat! Then you feel His cleansing power—shooting upward—toward your mind, your eyes, your ears and your tongue. Now you feel it speeding downward—toward your fingers and toes—purging, energizing and revitalizing as it goes. When the Spirit has finished His travels, you feel like a new person once again.

"Incredible!" you exclaim. "On a scale from one to ten, this experience scores a hundred!" I must remember to set aside more times like this one—times when I reflect on all the Spirit has done, is doing and will do. Wow!"

According to Charles Stanley, being still before God can "transform a life, metamorphose a mind, and reset purpose and direction for eternity. The sad heart is cheered, the confused mind is ordered, the pessimistic outlook is eliminated, the lonely spirit is befriended, the rebellious will is subdued, and the drifting seeker is made steadfast."[11] The drifting seeker is "steadfast" because he has been "filled" with God's Spirit, and he knows it.

However, should "the drifting seeker" take back control of any part of his body (eyes, ears, tongue, etc.) and do what he wants to do, rather than what the Spirit wants him to do, he will no longer be "filled." That is why the Bible refers to the Spirit's filling as a continuous process. "Keep being filled,"[12] it urges.

That also may be why evangelist D. L. Moody is reported to have answered as he did when asked why he prays again and again for the Spirit's filling. "Because I leak," he said.

We all "leak," my friend. We all have to stay in or close to the Source of water.

"The 'water' certainly has made a positive change in my life," you say. "I entered a totally foreign environment, yet I have never felt more at home. I raised the white flag of surrender, yet I am victorious in every way. I gave up more than I ever thought I could, yet I have received more than I knew was there. I died to my dreams, yet I am more alive than I ever dreamed possible.

"Why did I wait so long? Why did I fight so hard? Why did I doubt what God could do? If I had only known...."

You look toward your guide, who, by now, is out in the current. He is grinning. "You did well," he shouts. "You positioned yourself properly, you presented yourself to God, you proceeded forward, you remembered to praise God as you were advancing, and then you took the plunge. After you were in the water and had a chance to experience being wet all over, you paused to reflect on what the Spirit had done. Now I have a question. Are you ready for your first swimming lesson?"

"I guess I am," you shout back. "As ready as I'll ever be."

Notes

1. Henry T. Blackaby and Claude V. King, *Experiencing God* (Nashville: Broadman and Holman Publishers, 1994), p. 35.
2. C. S. Lewis, *The Silver Chair* (Indianapolis: The Macmillan Company, 1953), pp. 16-17.
3. Marguerite Reiss, *Holy Nudges* (Plainfield, N.J.: Logos International, 1976), p. 5.
4. Deuteronomy 8:7.
5. Andrew Murray, quoted by Susan Isbell Lugar in "Pressing On...the Story of Amy Carmichael," *Just Between Us* (Fall 1996): 23.
6. Romans 12:1.
7. Hebrews 10:5,7.
8. Joshua 3:8,15,16,17.
9. J. S. Bunting, *The Secret of a Quiet Mind* (London, England: Oliphant Ltd., 1956), p. 79.
10. Samuel M. Shoemaker, *With the Holy Spirit and With Fire* (New York: HarperCollins, 1960), p. 90.
11. Charles Stanley, *How to Listen to God* (Nashville: Thomas Nelson, Inc., 1985), p. 161.
12. See Ephesians 5:18.

PART FOUR:
Profound Implications

~~~~~~

"Indeed, not even half was told me."
1 Kings 10:7

15

From a Trickle to a Torrent

~~~~~~~~~~

Water will gush forth in the wilderness and streams in
the desert. The burning sand will become a pool, the
thirsty ground bubbling springs.

ISAIAH 35:6,7

All rivers begin small—with droplets of water from the heavens or from
melting snow. Together these drops form a trickle, which, farther down
the path, becomes a rill. This rill then turns into a stream, which eventually becomes deep enough and full enough to be dubbed a river. As it
rushes toward the sea, this torrent of water can be exciting to watch and
even more exciting to join.

Rivers start in mountains, usually in places that are remote, even
secret. By the time the water reaches the valley and the river has established an ecosystem, it begins drawing creatures and people in abundance. Mature rivers encourage activity.

In the process of aging, rivers change. When they are young and
vibrant, they channel through the earth's crust so forcefully that they
have no trouble at all breaking through barriers and carving deep
canyons. When they get older, though, rivers slow down a bit, drop
loads that are too heavy and then meander lazily around them. In the

process, they deposit some delightful surprises at the feet of those camping by their shores. Every stage of a river's life seems to have its benefits.

Sometimes a river overflows its banks. When this happens, people suffer loss. Yet considering all the devastation a flood can cause, it can also bring blessings. For the overflowing river deposits rich nutrients into soil that is impoverished, reclaiming it. Nobody wants a flood, but everybody likes the renewal that results. In a similar way, life in general can be overwhelming at times. Although none of us welcome crises, most of us recognize that these times of trial are when our greatest spiritual growth takes place.

Rivers, with all their stages and all their risks, are part of a well thought-out cycle. According to *National Geographic* (August 1980), "Each day the sun evaporates a trillion tons of water from the oceans and continents and pumps it as vapor into the atmosphere." There it remains until it returns to the earth as rain or snow. Then it may begin another river or join one already in progress. It is an incredibly efficient process.

Throughout the world, many rivers have formed. All are different. People gravitate toward the ones that interest them. When it comes to spiritual rivers, everybody gets caught up in one or another. Why not let it be *the* river, God's river, His...

RIVER OF DELIGHTS

"I see now what Ezekiel's river was (Ezekiel 47)," writes W. Glyn Evans, devotional author. "The river flowed from the temple with increasing depth—ankle-deep, knee-deep, loin-deep, then deep enough to swim. Lord, you want me to be a swimming Christian, abandoned to You in love so that I am carried away by it."[1] Indeed He does want us to be "carried away by it."

Once a person enters Ezekiel's river, he or she is in for the adventure of a lifetime. Imagine you are the type who loves a thrill. During your lifetime you have been on many rides. This ride, you decide, though, beats them all. You start off slowly, then SWISH! You feel yourself being swept by a torrent into a dark, highly walled canyon. Before you know it, you are being swept out again into a bright, open desert. "Ahhh!"

Riding the current, you find that you are in an excellent position to watch the river in action. It is an awesome force for good. You notice how it searches out things that are empty and fills them to overflowing. It encircles plants that look droopy and quickly perks them up. It builds up that which is depressed. It offers drink to the thirsty and food to the hungry. It transports necessities to those waiting to receive. It provides recreation for those too long without fun. It brings power to spots that were never connected. Some of these spots don't even know what power is. It would be exciting, you conclude, to watch the river do all these things without you. You are part of the action, however, and that is pure joy. You would never have believed you could love anything so much. "Praise the Lord!" you shout to nobody in particular.

> In an age when water is bottled
> and sold, it is refreshing to hear
> that the most valuable water
> of all is free.

You are amazed at your own reaction. You are relishing that which, before, you would have resisted. For example, you no longer fight for control of what is happening, yet you love the release your relinquishment brings. You have been swallowed by something much bigger than yourself, yet you don't mind being "absorbed."

On the contrary, you like the idea that when people come searching for you, they have to look into the river. At first they can't even find you. All they see is flowing water. When they do spot you, they are more interested in watching the water than in listening to you describe it. The whole situation seems incredible, yet you are happy—so happy that you would have joined the river sooner if you had known how great the experience would be. Much sooner.

As the river carries you along, you find yourself becoming both a recipient and a bestower of its blessings. You know you can't pour out, though, until you first take in. So you concentrate hard on...

THE RIVER'S INFLOW

The river serves many functions in your life, you discover—all of them beneficial. For example, you take swimming lessons and learn different strokes. In the process you end up swallowing water. It is so cool and pure and tastes so good that you might decide from now on the river will be your primary THIRST-QUENCHER.

You realize the Bible encourages such a decision: "Whoever is thirsty, let him come; and whoever wishes, let him take the free gift of the water of life."[2] In an age when water is bottled and sold, it is refreshing to hear that the most valuable water of all is free. *I want to partake of this water always*, you think as you cup your hand to your mouth.

The river also acts as your CLEANSER. It washes from you whatever dirt you pick up when you step onto its banks and venture into town. When you return from your wanderings and plunge in once again, it feels good to take a spiritual bath.

In the Bible you discover the apostle Paul talks not only about outer cleansing, but also of the inner "washing with water through the word."[3] You take that to mean that the Holy Spirit wants not only to immerse you in Himself, but in the Scriptures He penned as well. That way He can purify you thoroughly for whatever service He wants you to render. *Keep me clean*, you find yourself praying, *on the inside as well as on the outside. I want to be a vessel fit for the Master's use.*

Suddenly you look down. You see yourself in the water. *Oh no!* you wonder. *Is this the image I'm projecting to others? Worse yet, is this the way I look to God?* Maybe so. For the water is a MIRROR, showing us ourselves as we really are. Help!

The good news, however, is that this mirror can reflect our many moods. In some spots the river is quiet; in others it bubbles over with enthusiasm. In some places it is a trickle; in others it is a powerful force for change. Of the river's many faces, you can always seem to find one to match your present feelings. When you want to be still, you can choose a glassy spot. When you are restless, you can gravitate to a place where the river is cutting through new territory. Whatever part you select, it is comforting to know that the essence of the river never changes. It adapts to its many surroundings without ever compromising its nature. *I'm learning a valuable lesson*, you think.

Yes, you are. The river is your TEACHER. Amy Carmichael draws our attention to this particular function. Speaking of someone who became too caught up in the busyness of life, she writes, "One day as he sat by a mountain stream, he noticed the lovely way of water when interrupted by the boulders that broke its ordered flow....And he understood that it was possible to live the river's way if only he took the interrupting things, not as interruptions, but as opportunities, and indeed as very part of life."[4] *Holy Spirit of God, you pray, teach me to accept my interruptions, too, and turn them into divine appointments.*

} Holy Spirit of God,...teach me to
} accept my interruptions,...and turn
} them into divine appointments.

You would never have believed it a short while ago, but the river is now your main source of ENJOYMENT. You love to wade into it and let it cool you down. You like to splash it on your arms. Occasionally, in a burst of enthusiasm, you splash your companions, too. Those who are new to the river are almost always surprised by how refreshing it can be. You understand their reaction. You used to be right where they are, but no longer. You frolic in the water with the abandon of a little child now. You don't care what people think. You are "in the Spirit" and enjoying every moment of it.

You float, you dive and you practice every swimming stroke there is. Sometimes you get so bold you explore parts of the river that are new to you. Occasionally you get swept away by the current and find yourself in strange surroundings. Philip, after witnessing to the Ethiopian eunuch, had a similar experience when "the Spirit of the Lord suddenly took [him] away."[5] *God has quite a system of transport,* you conclude. *What a ride He offers to those who trust Him!*

You haven't been in the river very long, but already you consider it HOME. "I profoundly believe," says Samuel Shoemaker, "[that living in the 'stream of the Holy Spirit'] is the native climate for a Christian, as much as water is the natural element for a fish."[6] You agree. *At last I'm where I was meant to be. I have a sense of belonging, but nobody could have told me my new home would be in an area I was formerly afraid of!*

In addition to all these other functions, the river provides INSPIRA-TION. You especially enjoy visiting its source. You like climbing to the spot where heaven links itself to earth—to the spot where the river of life has its beginning at the foot of the Sovereign's throne. You love to listen to the King as He gives His directives to the river—directives that reverberate throughout the world.

"Flow, river, flow!" you hear the Father command the Spirit. "Overcome every obstacle in your path. Satisfy the thirsty. Feed the hungry. Fill up the empty. Wash the dirty. Soften the hard hearted. Strengthen the weak. Revitalize the weary. Cool down those who are feverish. Lift up those who have sinking spirits. River, do what I have empowered you to do. And do it well." At the conclusion of these words you pray: *Lord God, You are a magnificent Sovereign. I am overwhelmed by Your power and Your love.*

You are not alone in your praise. W. Glyn Evans shares similar sentiments. "That is what You did for me, Lord," he writes, "when I first heard Your name and gave my heart to You. The barren wilderness became green as the water of life started to trickle through my life. Fruit and flowers began to grow, and people began to notice and comment on them."[7] This was Evans's indication that he should start focusing on...

THE SPIRIT'S OUTFLOW

Jesus said, "'If anyone is thirsty, let him come to me and drink. Whoever believes in me, as the Scripture has said, streams of living water will flow from within him.' By this he meant the Spirit."[8]

Outflow is a necessity. You know that. You remember Oswald Chambers saying, "If you satisfy yourself with a blessing from God, it will corrupt you; you must sacrifice it, pour it out, do with it what common sense says is an absurd waste."[9]

That is what people said about Mary's act of breaking her alabaster jar of perfume and rubbing the expensive scent on Jesus' head. "'Why this waste?' they asked." But it wasn't a waste to Jesus. He said, "'She has done a beautiful thing to me.'"[10] *I want to do beautiful things for You, too, Lord Jesus,* you pray. *To pour out has become my heart's desire.*

Serving isn't easy. It wasn't easy for Jesus either. When He set about washing His disciples' feet, He faced challenges. One came from Judas, who accepted the Master's gesture of love, then later turned against Him.

Ouch! That hurt! Another challenge came from Peter, who at first didn't want to be served; but, after learning he needed to be, tried to get Jesus to do more than was necessary.[11] Oh, the frustration! *Sometimes you can't win when you reach out to people,* you figure, *but I want to do it anyway.*

Why? The rewards far outweigh the risks. Most of the time the return on an investment surpasses anything you might have anticipated. Perhaps that is what the Spirit meant when He promised, "A generous man will prosper; he who refreshes others will himself be refreshed."[12] *I believe it,* you whisper to the Lord. *Nobody can outgive You.*

You have become so lost in your thoughts you don't realize you are not the only one riding the river's current. Others are doing the same. When you do notice them, you are struck by...

The Amazing
Creativity of the Spirit

The way the Spirit works in each individual life is unique. "When the Holy Spirit is poured out upon God's people, their experiences will differ widely," says Watchman Nee. "Some will receive new vision, others will know a new liberty in soul winning, others will proclaim the Word of God with fresh power, and yet others will be filled with heavenly joy and overflowing praise."[13] As each learns to respect the other's experiences, the whole Body of believers enjoys new vitality.

Although the Holy Spirit is unique in His dealings with individuals, all believers share some of the same blessings. They all have a heightened awareness of the Spirit's workings in their lives. Their eyes have been opened, their ears unclogged and their tongues set free to praise the Savior's name. Their broken hearts are mending, their tightly clasped hands are holding things more loosely and their arms are starting to reach out, even to the unlovely. *I wouldn't have missed this experience for anything!* you tell the Lord. *Thank You, thank You, thank You for including me.*

As you travel "in the Spirit" with these other believers, you become more and more appreciative that you are all in this together, that you are part of a larger organism, known as the Body of Christ. In this Body all of you have different functions. Some have been incorporated as "minds"; they are the ones gifted by the Spirit to administrate, organize and lead. Others are "eyes," given ability to envision what most people cannot see. Still others are "ears," especially equipped for listening. Some are "noses," endowed with an ability to sniff out problems. Some are "mouths," Christians who have the gift of articulating praise through song or the spoken word.

As your focus shifts to the "torso" of the Body, you become aware of the vital functions of the "hearts." These are people who have been filled with an extra measure of compassion and love. You also notice the "hands," those empowered to reach out to the needy, to touch the brokenhearted and to heal the emotionally, spiritually or physically ill. As you come to the "loins," you thank the Spirit for people He has commissioned to reproduce the Body with boldness and effectiveness.

Moving to the lower extremities, you come to the "knees," pray-ers who approach the throne of grace with confidence because the Spirit has merged their wills into His. Last, you notice the "feet," Christians who have been energized by the Spirit to go into local neighborhoods, schools, offices, plants, hospitals or to mission fields farther away, going with the express purpose of presenting the good news of Jesus Christ.

As you meditate upon the diversity in this Body of Christ, you are aware that each individual first had to present his or her own body to the Spirit. The Spirit then immersed it and sovereignly incorporated it into the larger Body. *We are all part of a carefully orchestrated plan,* you acknowledge to the Lord. *Now enable us to function well together so that others will want to join us.*

Suddenly you are jarred out of your meditation by a shout. You recognize it as coming from your guide. He is on the crest of the same wave. "Enjoying yourself?" he asks.

"You know I am," you shout back.

"Ready to search out some treasure?"

"You bet!"

"Then follow me," he beckons as he swims to a quieter part of the river. "I'll show you where to look. The author wants to get in on the excitement, too. So listen to her as she tells you a story."

Notes

1. W. Glyn Evans, *Daily With the King* (Chicago: Moody Press, 1979), p. 45.
2. Revelation 22:17.
3. Ephesians 5:26.
4. Amy Carmichael, *His Thoughts Said, His Father Said* (Fort Washington, Pa.: Christian Literature Crusade, n.d.), p. 39.
5. See Acts 8:39.
6. Samuel M. Shoemaker, *With the Holy Spirit and With Fire* (New York: HarperCollins, 1960), p. 14.
7. Evans, *Daily With the King*, p. 33.
8. John 7:37-39.
9. Oswald Chambers, *My Utmost for His Highest* (New York: Dodd, Mead, and Company, 1935), p. 247.
10. See Matthew 26:6-13.
11. See John 13:9.
12. Proverbs 11:25.
13. Watchman Nee, *The Normal Christian Life* (Fort Washington, Pa.: Christian Literature Crusade, 1963), p. 97.

16

Treasures in the Sand

～～～～～

"They will feast on the abundance of the seas,
on the treasures hidden in the sand."
DEUTERONOMY 33:19

I was standing with three of my grandchildren by the ocean in front of our high-rise. We were watching efforts to reclaim our badly eroded beach. Out in the sea, a dredging ship was sucking up a mixture of sand and water from the ocean's bottom, then spraying the sludge out of a huge pipe, the mouth of which was located not far from us. As the pipe disgorged its contents, out came some beautiful shells.

The children decided to go "treasure hunting." Looking for something unusual is half the fun, you know, and finding it, pure ecstasy.

"Gram Gram, look at this!" seven-year-old Jessica shouted as she ran toward me, clutching a sand dollar.

"Beautiful!" I exclaimed. "Those are rare around here."

Her younger sister, Valerie, held up a similar find and shook it near my ear.

"I hear 'doves' inside," I remarked. "If you want to, we can let them out."

"I think I found a shark's tooth!" Mark interrupted, as he squeezed a black rectangular shape between his little thumb and forefinger.

"I think you did, Mark. Great find!"

That afternoon we discussed the ocean's many treasures, some of which are quite valuable. We also discovered, courtesy of our encyclopedia, that rivers and streams produce treasures, too. In fact, the largest nugget of gold ever found came from a streambed in Australia. It weighed in at a whopping 248 pounds! In order to find such "jewels," though, it takes perseverance, because the best treasures are often down deep. To bring them to the surface, one has to...

PROBE THE DEPTHS

You are still with your mentor in the swift-flowing current. By this time you have learned to swim pretty well, so you are now preparing for your first diving expedition. You know that the best treasures are located beneath you, in the deepest part of the river, so that is where you intend to search.

C. S. Lewis describes what you will be experiencing: "One may think of a diver," he writes, "first reducing himself to nakedness, then glancing mid-air, then gone with a splash, vanished, rushing down through green and warm water, down through the increasing pressure into the deathlike region of ooze and slime and old decay; then up again, back to colour and light, his lungs almost bursting, till suddenly he breaks surface again, holding in his hand the dripping, precious thing that he went down to recover."[1]

Just as there are deep things of a physical nature, "There are deep things of God," F. B. Meyer says, "mysteries, hidden things, of which the apostle Paul often speaks. Deeper than...the fathomless depths beneath, they defy the wise and prudent of the world. But they are revealed to babes...through the grace of the Holy Spirit."[2]

Not only is it the Spirit's job to reveal these "hidden things," but it is also His job to bring them to the surface. "I sometimes think of the Holy Spirit as a deep sea diver who goes to the depths searching for treasures," Charles Swindoll says. "Sometimes, the treasures are so precious, they are priceless. Without the diver, however, they would remain hidden forever."[3]

Now this sounds confusing, I know, for up till this time we have been thinking of the Holy Spirit as the "water" in which we are swimming. Now we are being told He is a "diver," bringing up precious treasures. You are probably asking, *Is the Holy Spirit both? If so, what am I?*

> Think of [the Holy Spirit] as leading you deeper into the things of God, which is the same as leading you deeper into Himself.

Think of yourself as a "diving suit," that which the Spirit indwells as He plunges to the depths. Think of Him as surrounding you and filling you, both at the same time. Think of Him as leading you deeper into the things of God, which is the same as leading you deeper into Himself.

At times the Holy Spirit will lead you so deep that you hit the bedrock that lies underneath the river. That Rock, you will discover, is Christ, the One "in whom are hidden all the treasures of wisdom and knowledge."[4]

You will have a hard time finding words to describe the thrill of probing the mysteries of the Savior—the mysteries of His pre-incarnation, His virgin birth, His sinless life, His substitutionary death, His astonishing resurrection, His spectacular ascension, His being seated at the right hand of God the Father and His eventual return to earth in power and glory. If you choose to delve into such studies, though, the worth will be inestimable.

Spiritual diving expeditions, however, are rarely easy. They require hours of Bible study, which at times can be quite tedious, coupled with dogged persistence in prayer—prayer that seems to be producing no fruit at all. It may help to remember this is the way it is in physical diving expeditions as well. Months of fruitless searching may be necessary before a treasure is found. When one is, it's worth the wait. "WOW! Look what I found!" the diver exclaims. "Feast your eyes on this incredible jewel!"

Sometimes, though, a treasure is so awesome that it simply cannot be shared, not with anybody. To even try would seem to diminish its worth. That was the case with Mary, the mother of Jesus. After she had given birth to the long-awaited Messiah, she looked down at the precious baby in her arms, contemplated the future, and became overwhelmed with emotion. Talking about her hopes and fears was impossible. So she "treasured up all these things," the Bible says, "and pondered them in her heart."[5]

Whether shared or stored, though, there are spiritual treasures to be had. So let's discuss the best hunting grounds. The first is...

THE BIBLE

Some days, when you are having your daily devotions in the Word of God, all of a sudden a verse from another location may pop into your head. When you look it up, you find it enriches the original passage. This is SUPERNATURAL GUIDANCE, the directing of the Holy Spirit to verses He wants you to assimilate.

The late Eugenia Price, author of many books, had such an experience. She says, "There began a leading of the Holy Spirit through the Scriptures, to one surprising spot and then another, some of which I couldn't have found otherwise without a concordance."[6]

Other Christians testify to experiencing a somewhat different phenomenon. Charles Stanley is one of them. "[The Holy Spirit] knows how to make a verse bear witness with your human spirit," he says. "He knows how to make a verse leap off the page and into your life."[7]

The "leap-off-the-page" part of Stanley's testimony is what I call SUPERNATURAL MAGNIFICATION, the Spirit's ability to emphasize the meaning of a text. The "into-your-life" part I dub SUPERNATURAL ILLUMINATION, that certain connection from Spirit to spirit that makes one say, "I see it! Now I'll do it!"

LISTEN TO A STORY FROM THE AUTHOR

My husband, Lee, and I love to go on treasure hunts in God's Word. Let me tell you about one of our finds. I'll give you some background information first to help you understand the situation. We had become members of a church, which, at the time of our joining, had a born-again pastor, lots of lay involvement, and, therefore, multiple opportunities to serve.

One day we learned, to our horror, that our godly leader had been forced out by the "powers to be" and was to be replaced by a man whose character, theology and motives were being questioned by some of our fellow members. We investigated and found the situation to be much worse, even, than we had been told. What to do? Resign immediately or stay and try to make changes?

We dove into God's Word, believing that from its limitless resources we would find the answer to our dilemma. We did. Where in God's Word we found it, however, was amazing. You see, we had been systematically reading through the Bible, tackling a chapter or two a day. On the day we learned of the church's upheaval, we were scheduled to be in the Old Testament book of 1 Samuel, chapter 11. As I glanced at the title, "Saul Rescues the City of Jabesh," I thought to myself, *There certainly won't be any advice for us in this obscure passage!*

How wrong I was! The passage told of an "enemy" who was threatening to subject the Israelites to conditions their God could never approve. The Israelites faced a choice: fight the enemy or surrender without a fight. If they chose to fight without asking for help, they, being a minority, would probably lose. On the other hand, if they signed the peace treaty the enemy was proposing, they would be compromising the principles God had given them.

They made their decision. They would sign the treaty. No war for them. They wanted peace—and they wanted it at any price. Then they learned how high the price was. Their right eyes, the treaty specified, were to be gouged out. Now they would not only suffer great pain, but also their vision would be limited, making it hard for them to protect themselves in future battles.

When Saul heard of their plan to compromise, he "burned with anger," the Bible says. He took oxen, cut them into pieces and scattered them throughout Israel. This was a traditional call to battle. As Lee and I read about this butchering, though, we saw it as more. We saw it as a warning of the division that would come to God's people if they refused to fight for what was right—division that would not only destroy their effectiveness as a church, but would "stink" in the nostrils of their holy God.

So Lee put down his Bible, sat down at his desk and wrote a letter to the board, pleading with them to reconsider the man they were about to hire. Lee lost the battle. The board decided to stick by its original decision.

"O God," we prayed, "this church is no longer something we feel comfortable being identified with, but we have friends here. To withdraw our membership might strain those relationships. It would also require us to give up teaching our Bible class. That would be like losing a loved one. But, Lord, we cannot compromise our convictions. You know that. What do You want us to do?" By the time we came to these last words, our eyes were moist.

> Hannah cried out to the Lord. In
> so doing, she discovered treasures
> in praising, treasures in petitioning
> and the treasure of peace.

A couple of difficult days passed. We continued to read 1 Samuel. Then it happened. We came to chapter 16. "How long will you mourn?" the Scripture asked. "Fill your horn with oil and be on your way;...I will show you what to do."

Talk about supernatural guidance, magnification and illumination! All were there—in huge, convicting letters, direct from the pen of our Helper.

"Spirit of the living God, You have spoken," we exclaimed. "Now keep us faithful to obey."

We followed through on our commitment to God's Spirit by withdrawing our membership. The direction the church took after that confirmed, to us at least, that we had made the right decision. The cost was high, however. Friendships were strained, and we lost our Bible study group. In the midst of the turmoil, though, we discovered some valuable treasures. We received the joy of God's abiding presence; the direction of our personal Helper, His Holy Spirit; peace concerning our decision; and a holy boldness to articulate our convictions. We also found a new church—one thoroughly grounded in the Word of God.

We are still amazed, however, that the Spirit could speak to us through such an obscure passage of Scripture. We feel we can say with John Bunyan of old, "I never had in all my life so great an inlet into the Word of God as now: those Scriptures that I saw nothing in before are made...to shine before me."[8]

Such an experience can belong to any of us if we are faithful in our

Bible reading—faithful to the point of being willing to go through parts that are tedious—parts that look as if they have nothing to offer.

Now let's talk about how to find treasures in...

PRAYER

This is where Hannah, wife of Elkanah, did her treasure hunting. We find her story in that same "obscure" book of 1 Samuel. Frustrated by her inability to bear children, Hannah cried out to the Lord. In so doing, she discovered treasures in praising, treasures in petitioning and the treasure of peace. Let's examine her treasures one at a time.

We all know hearts are lifted through PRAISE, so it is not surprising that Hannah began her prayer with "O Lord Almighty," a phrase of exaltation. It is also not surprising that by the time she finished, "her face was no longer downcast."

Other treasures come through PETITION. As Hannah verbalized her request, she discovered that her burden was being lifted. That was a treasure in itself. Nine months later, however, an even more valuable treasure appeared: a son. She testified, "I prayed for this child, and the Lord...granted me what I asked of him."[9]

Now we don't want to be guilty of associating the word "treasures" with getting what we ask of the Lord—and only that. Sometimes the best treasures of all lie in answers that are not what we requested. These treasures can be, however, hard to see. Mystified, we cry out, *What has the Spirit done? Given me a stone when I asked for bread?*

Curious, we examine our "stone." Suddenly we spot a nondescript glassy nodule. We rush to an appraiser. There we learn that our "stone" contains a valuable diamond. We are humbled—and grateful—that God's ways are not our ways. We resolve to remember the lesson we have learned, that "non-answers" can be the most precious answers of all.

A third treasure to be found in prayer is PEACE. It comes, the Bible reminds us, as we "present [our] requests to God."[10] It comes in the midst of circumstances that are anything but peaceful. Consider Hannah.

Or a Christian who has just discovered a spouse's infidelity and knows that divorce is now a real option.

Or one who is about to go to court to win custody of his or her children.

Or one who has just dropped off a teenager at the freshman dorm of a university and smells pot being smoked down the hall.

Or one whose reputation has been compromised by the malicious gossip of so-called friends.

Or one who has to make a difficult decision regarding parental care and doesn't know what to do.

Or one who has been thrust into an uncomfortable spotlight and discovers he or she is expected to provide leadership.

Or one who was pink-slipped at work today.

Or one who is being wheeled into an operating room for major surgery.

Or one who has just learned of a loved one's death.

> The most valuable treasure
> to be found in prayer,...is
> the wonder of simply being
> in the presence of God.

These Christians can indeed find peace, but only if they go to God in prayer. For along with Bible study, prayer is a rich hunting ground for spiritual treasure.

The most valuable treasure to be found in prayer, however, is not in any of the aforementioned things. It is the wonder of simply being in the presence of God. There we can gaze upon His radiant face. There we can experience the warmth of His touch and the depth of His love. There we also know that even at that very moment, His Spirit is working to turn our earthly burdens into something of eternal value. What riches!

Now let's consider one more field where we can sometimes find a jewel:

LIFE'S MUNDANE CIRCUMSTANCES

It helps to remember that the Holy Spirit is with us as we go about our daily routines. In fact, if we are looking, He will be revealing nuggets of truth to us all day long. For example, we can discover a treasure every time we realize...

- God is interested in how my job is going.
- His Spirit can bring joy into my daily grind.
- His Spirit can turn my interruptions into opportunities, even into divine appointments.
- His Spirit can funnel me in the right direction by closing and opening doors.
- His Spirit can enable me to look beyond the chaos of the moment into the calmness of the future.
- His Spirit can turn evil into good and curses into blessings.
- His Spirit can meet me in my tragedies and draw me closer to Himself.

These are treasures, my friend. They are there for the taking. They have been provided so that we may go through life as more than just survivors. We can become adventurers—on the quest of a lifetime.

We have to remember, of course, that not all spiritual treasures are meant to be discovered. Some are locked within God's secret will. For example, no matter how earnestly we ask Him to reveal the reasons why certain things happen, He may not do it. Other things He will reveal. These other things, the Bible says, "belong to us and to our children forever."[11] One of the treasures that *is* revealed is the way of fishermen casting their nets.

"There's a spot downriver where folks are bringing in big catches," your guide says. "Want to search it out?"

"Let's go," you reply. "I absolutely *love* the things I am learning. I don't want to miss a single lesson."

Notes
1. C. S. Lewis, *Miracles* (Indianapolis: The Macmillan Company, 1947), p. 116.
2. F. B. Meyer, *Daily Meditations* (Dallas, Tex.: Word Books, 1979), March 30.
3. Charles Swindoll, *Living Closer to the Flame* (Dallas, Tex.: Word Publishing, 1993), p. 103.
4. Colossians 2:3.

5. Luke 2:19.

6. Quoted by V. Raymond Edman, *They Found the Secret* (Grand Rapids: Zondervan Publishing House, 1960), p. 116.

7. Charles Stanley, *The Wonderful Spirit-Filled Life* (Nashville: Thomas Nelson Publishers, 1992), p. 218.

8. Quoted by V. Raymond Edman, *They Found the Secret*, p. 34.

9. Hannah's story is found in 1 Samuel 1:1-28.

10. Philippians 4:6.

11. Deuteronomy 29:29.

Full Nets

They were unable to haul the net in
because of the large number of fish.

JOHN 21:6

Are you ready for another visit to the author's high rise on the Atlantic Ocean? I am inviting you to come today because "the blues are running," as fisherfolk say. Pull a chair close to the window, grab a pair of binoculars, look at the water and tell me what you see. Boats? Lots and lots of them? All jockeying for position?

Now, scan the waves until you see a spot exploding with activity. Find one? The frantic splashing you are observing is created, I have been told, by bait fish. They are leaping out of the water to escape the jaws of the bluefish. You will notice that whenever a new area of frenzy appears, the boats gravitate toward it. It is the summons to a good catch.

You will soon realize that from your perspective, you have an advantage over the people in the boats. You can see the bigger picture. Because of that, you are going to want to shout, "Over here! There's a good fishing spot over here!"

If you do, though, you won't get any response. Not unless the boaters look your way or tune in to your "wavelength." Too bad. For you could lead them to areas where fish are waiting to be caught. It would be even better, you realize, if you could direct the fish to the boaters.

Keeping this picture in your mind, put yourself...

ON THE SHORE OF THE SEA OF TIBERIAS

Jesus is standing there in a postresurrection appearance. His disciples, you remember, are fishing on this lake. At first they don't recognize the Stranger on the beach. Then He shouts, "Having any success?"

"None," they indicate.

"Throw your net on the right side of the boat," Jesus commands. When they do, "they [are] unable to haul the net in," the Bible says, "because of the large number of fish."[1]

This amazing story requires some probing. What made the disciples successful the second time around?

Did they change location? No. They stayed in the very same spot—a spot that was teeming with fish.

Did they change technique? No. They had been using the same technique for years and would continue to use it for many more.

Did they change crew? No. It was the same crew—a crew as qualified as any other to bring in a huge catch.

What, then, made the difference? They stopped relying on themselves and started to rely on Someone standing on the shore; Someone positioned to see the bigger picture; Someone who could redirect the fish to where they were fishing. To be successful, though, they had to look to Him, listen to Him and obey Him. When they did, they caught fish.

This account has just as much application today as it did two thousand years ago, because Jesus is calling us now, as He called His disciples back then, to become...

FISHERS OF MEN

Let's expand our water analogy for a moment. Instead of thinking of the river as the Person of the Holy Spirit and only that, let's enlarge it to include the Spirit's plan to bring pre-Christians to a saving knowledge of Jesus Christ. An abundance of "fish" are present in the river. They just need people to "catch" them—people who are willing to take their directions from the Omniscient One on the shore.

For those who respond to the Lord's advice, fishing for souls can be more exciting, even, than fishing for fish. "I would rather fish for men," quips Dr. D. James Kennedy of Evangelism Explosion, "because when I catch them, God cleans them."

It is easy to agree with Kennedy, for it is nice to have Someone do the dirty work, especially when that Someone does such a good job of it. Cleaning fish, however, is of little concern to a person who has never fished before. That person may be more worried about stepping into a boat.

It is hard to obey God, especially when risk is involved, but the results can be quite marvelous. Let me mention a few. When we follow Christ's lead, we, like the disciples, may discover...

A MISSION FIELD
RIGHT WHERE WE ARE

Fish can be caught everywhere the river runs. It runs by our homes, through our neighborhoods, past our schools, offices, plants, hospitals, government buildings and churches. This river is "teeming with creatures beyond number—living things both large and small."[2] These "living things" come in all shapes and sizes. They come in a variety of colors, too. Not only are the "blues" running, but so are the reds, the yellows, the blacks, the whites and the browns. According to Ezekiel's vision, even the Dead Sea will become a good fishing spot.

That may seem impossible because we know the Dead Sea has more toxic salt than any body of water on earth, but when the river of life runs through it, the Dead Sea "becomes fresh."

Ezekiel adds, "There will be large numbers of fish."[3] So next time you are in an environment that is corrupt, and you think, *God will never be able to do anything here*, take heart. The river of life may be running through that place. Fish may just be waiting to leap into your net.

Another exciting result of following the Savior's directions is a new awareness of...

WHO WE ARE IN CHRIST

Think about it. We, who were an impure people, are now indwelt by a Spirit who is holy. We, who were a weak generation, are now empowered by a God whose abilities are limitless. We, who were a fallen nation, have been lifted to the heights of heaven. Think about how advantageous is our positioning as Christians. We know both worlds: God's and ours. Who is better qualified to reach people with the message of eternal life than we are?

Introducing earth-bound people to heavenly things, however, requires wisdom. For there is danger in leaning too far in either direction. "Some Christians are close to God but remote from people," Samuel Shoemaker says. "Some are close to people but remote from God. Some are close to neither; and some are close to both. Of these last come the real 'fishers of men.'"[4]

> Fishing for souls is natural for the Holy Spirit. He can reveal the right approach and supply the right words to those who are sensitive to His leading.

Some of us are afraid that if we get close to people and realize we are their link to eternal life—perhaps their only link—the thought might be overwhelming. It could make us reluctant to speak up at all, for fear we might mess up. This is a valid concern, but that is where our Helper comes in. He reminds us that wherever we are, He has placed us there, and He has done so with a purpose. He will not let that purpose be thwarted. He wants us to open our mouths in readiness. Then He will present the gospel through us with power and conviction.

In addition, the Holy Spirit will teach us...

HOW TO FISH NATURALLY

We are talking now about shunning techniques that seem manipulative and relying totally on the Spirit to provide a more natural approach to fishing for souls. It is not that gimmicks never work. The Spirit can sometimes use a gimmick, but He knows a better way.

Spurgeon tells the story of three gentlemen who "went into New York and bought the best rods and lines that could be purchased, and they found out the exact fly for the particular day or month so that the fish might bite at once...." Then "they fished and fished and fished the live-long day, but the basket was empty...." Spurgeon continues, "A ragged boy came down from the hills....He had a bit of bough pulled off a tree, and a piece of string, and a bent pin; he put a worm on it, threw it in, and out came a fish directly....They asked him how he did it. And, he said...it was easy enough when you had the way of it."[5]

Fishing for souls is natural for the Holy Spirit. He can reveal the right approach and supply the right words to those who are sensitive to His leading. Nellie Pickard, author of several books about witnessing, writes, "When certain things are said to me, my spiritual radar rings in my ear. The Holy Spirit gives me a nudge. I follow the opening in the conversation and speak up for the Lord."[6] Oh, to obey this nudge!

The Spirit's nudge usually leads a Christian to present the gospel in the context of the listener's thinking. For example, we may be led to approach a financier about making an investment that is eternal. Or we may want to share with an electrician about plugging into the Light of the world. Or we may suggest to a builder that we all need a firm Foundation for life! The Spirit may also suggest an approach that is highly creative, such as the following one, which could be presented to an environmentalist interested in studying rivers:

"How would you like to hear about the world's most fascinating river? You won't find it on any map, but it's more real and more powerful than any physical river you've ever known. I discovered it when I was visiting a friend. The river was running through my friend's town. I wanted to get close enough to examine the water, but the river's banks were too high.

"One day, when I was alone, I found a place where access to the river was easy. The only trouble was, the access lay inside a walled park. This park had an entrance fee, and I didn't have any money. I stood at the gate, wondering what to do.

"Suddenly Someone approached, identified Himself, and said He knew my friend. He offered to pay my way into the park. I was thrilled but cautious. Then the Stranger assured me there were no strings attached. All I had to do was to take from Him a token, insert it into the turnstile, and it would click me in.

"I took the token, entered the park, approached the river, and waded in. It was the most amazing body of water I had ever seen. It provided me with relaxation, inspiration, good food, pure drink, valuable treasures, and great transportation. Then I discovered where it leads—past a hill called calvary and eventually to heaven's door. When I realized that, I knew I had to leave the river to tell people like you about it.

"If you are interested in exploring it, I can introduce you to the One who has the token. His name is Jesus the Christ. Meeting Him is a prerequisite to entering the 'water.'"

NOW WHAT?

Once we have mastered the knack of creating an approach to the gospel, we need to think about when to pursue someone and when to back off. When fishing, it is possible to move the rod too forcefully, causing the bait to move unnaturally. The fish, then, won't bite. Ian Thomas, the author, testifies to having had this problem of trying to coerce people

> Fishing for souls should be natural, but it should also be fun. So relax.

into becoming Christians. "Out of a sheer desire to win souls, to go out and get them," he admits, "I was a windmill of activity....The only thing that alarmed me was that nobody was converted!" Then Thomas decided to back off and let the Holy Spirit be the active One. The results were thrilling. "For five weeks, almost every day," he says, "people were converted."[7] Amazing!

Fishing for souls should be natural, but it should also be fun. So relax. After all, "'All that the Father gives...will come,'"[8] the Bible says. So anticipate success. Then watch the Holy Spirit make it happen.

Knowing you have relinquished control can bring a sense of release. You won't feel guilty when your fish gets away. For you know the Spirit has positioned other fishermen farther down the riverbank. One of those others is designated to bring your fish in. This was the case with me, the author. Be encouraged as I relate...

MARGEE'S STORY

When we lived in Massachusetts, I began a home Bible study for my neighbors. Margee, a member of the League of Women Voters and the local Episcopal church, attended the study whenever she could. She seemed to get nervous, however, whenever the discussion centered on a personal relationship with God through faith in Jesus Christ. When we were transferred to Michigan and the study came to a necessary end, I thought I had lost a fish.

Indeed I had, but God had not. His Holy Spirit was pursuing Margee, and He would catch her on someone else's line. This is how I learned of her exciting story:

One day, 15 or so years after Margee and I had lost contact, I went to the mailbox and found a letter showing her return address. By this time, I had become a lecturer on the Christian speaking circuit and had authored *Yet Will I Trust Him* (Regal Books). The book had been featured in several magazines, but I was thinking of none of that as I excitedly ripped open the envelope.

Having obtained Margee's permission, I will share, for the sake of discouraged fisherfolk everywhere, a portion of what she said:

Peggy—

Thank God I have found you....For almost ten years I have been praying off and on that I would find out where you and Lee are—I've wanted to share with you that both Jim and I (and our three children) have come to know Jesus as our personal Savior and Lord.

We know you prayed for us and I just wanted to let you know that the seeds you planted in my life so many years ago...have been fed and watered and finally sprouted....

At a point in my life when I was realizing that neither I nor the League of Women Voters had the answers, our minister began to speak about Jesus "the way Peggy used to." I began to read the Bible again, and the scales fell off my eyes and God renewed my mind, and I believed and was able to make a public confession, which made all the difference. Meanwhile, others among the "frozen chosen," began to exhibit an amazing love (amazing for Episcopalians, that is), which witnessed to Jim and he also was hooked.

Our life has not been problem free, of course. Your book really ministered—but through all the crises...the Lord has brought Jim and me closer together and many blessings have come.

Anyway, your book was quoted from in *Decision* magazine

earlier this year and I've since then been trying to track it down, being sure that Peg Rankin is probably Peggy Rankin, who lovingly and patiently presented the claims of Jesus, made me uncomfortable enough in my nominal Christianity to be open to the possibility that there really is something more....Found a bookstore that would order it for me, picked it up today, read it, and praise God.

Funny thing is, I've always been sure that some time our paths would cross again. If you are ever in Northern New Jersey, please call us....

God bless you all.

        Love,

        Margee

As I laid the letter on the kitchen table, a chill ran down my spine. *Holy Spirit of the living God,* I prayed, *thank You. Thank You for finishing what You began in my friend Margee's life. And thank You for touching her entire family with Your redemptive love. Thank You, too, for letting me know about it. What an Encourager You are!*

Then I thought, *Margee now lives in New Jersey. We are being transferred to New Jersey! We'll get together and praise our Lord in unison!*

Well, that's exactly what we did; and the joy of that special evening still warms my heart.

There's no question about it,...

GOD'S RIVER IS ON THE MOVE

God's river has flowed through the history of the world and will continue to flow until time is no more.

Directed by Jehovah Himself, it flowed through Abraham, who became the spiritual father of millions. It continued to flow through Jacob, who produced the 12 tribes of Israel; then on through Moses, who led God's people to the "Promised Land"; after that, it flowed through the prophets, who predicted a coming Messiah.

Into this stream of spiritual happenings, Jesus, the Promised One, stepped. He invited some disciples to join Him, and the stream started to flow through them. As the Holy Spirit continued to touch lives, "the Lord added to their number daily," the Bible says, "those who were being saved."[9] The river was clearly growing wider.

As it continued to flow through history, sweeping seekers into its life-changing current, the river met opposition. Powerful groups tried to deter its influence by killing, torturing and maiming those under its influence. "Stop these believers in Jesus Christ!" they shouted. "Put an end to this sect called Christianity!"

Nobody can stop the Holy Spirit of God, however. In fact, attempts to dam up the river made it run stronger than ever. On and on it flowed, through the decline of the Roman Empire, down through the Middle Ages, on through the Renaissance, the Age of Reason, the Industrial Revolution and the Age of Technology. Now, here it is, entering the Information Age, bursting onto the Internet and showing more potential than ever of reaching the world with the claims of Christ.

What an exciting age in which to be alive! Truly we can say with Stuart Briscoe, author-pastor, "From the beginning to the end of human history, there is a flowing from God, a river of blessing that has brought, does bring, and will bring the overflow of God to the world of men."[10]

"How thrilling to be part of such a life-changing force," you say to your mentor as the two of you are being swept along.

"Yes," he agrees, "and to have at our disposal all the river has to offer. Before long we'll be passing some fruit trees. Ready for a bite to eat?"

"Am I ready?! I'm ravenous! Let's take a break and sample what those trees over there on the bank have to offer."

Notes
1. John 21:6.
2. Psalm 104:25.
3. Ezekiel 47:8,9.
4. Samuel M. Shoemaker, *With the Holy Spirit and With Fire* (New York: HarperCollins, 1960), p. 70.

5. Charles Haddon Spurgeon, *The Soul Winner* (Grand Rapids: Wm. B. Eerdmans Publishing Company, 1963), p. 13.
6. Nellie Pickard, *What Do You Say When* (Grand Rapids: Baker Book House, 1988), p. 13.
7. W. Ian Thomas, as quoted by V. Raymond Edman in *They Found the Secret* (Grand Rapids: Zondervan Publishing House, 1960), p. 139.
8. John 6:37.
9. Acts 2:47.
10. Stuart Briscoe, *All Things Weird and Wonderful* (Wheaton, Ill.: Victor Books, 1977), p. 161.

Fruit for All Seasons

On each side of the river stood the tree of life, bearing
twelve crops of fruit, yielding its fruit every month.
REVELATION 22:2

"Look at those pear trees!" you exclaim to your teacher as the current
carries you two along the bank of the river.

"This is a good place to go ashore," he decides. So the two of you make
your way to the river's edge and climb up. "It's amazing," your mentor
comments, "this area was once a wilderness. Now that there's a river running through it, it's producing all this beautiful fruit!"

He picks a pear and offers it to you. You take a bite. Juice runs down
your chin. "Excellent!" you remark. "The best pear I ever had!"

GOOD FRUIT

is a sign that the tree from which it comes has healthy channels between
its trunk and its branches. It has a good system through which sap can
move effectively. The same thing is true in the Christian life. The fruit of
the Spirit, which the Bible describes as being "love, joy, peace, longsuf-

fering, gentleness, goodness, faithfulness, meekness and self-control,"[1] is evidence that a Christian is well connected to Jesus Christ and is allowing His Spirit to work.

"The Holy Spirit is the life-sap," says Andrew Murray, "through which the vine and the branches grow into real and living oneness."[2]

The big challenge for the Christian is to concentrate on preserving this "oneness," rather than getting diverted into trying to produce better fruit. I was introduced to this challenge when we lived in Michigan. The property on which our home was situated sported pear trees. Each spring those trees would burst into glorious bloom. Their bloom was a promise that there would be a harvest. We were never disappointed.

One day as I was admiring a pear, I came to a revealing conclusion: the trees that were providing this beautiful fruit didn't seem to be "working at it." They weren't in a frenzy trying to speed up production. I never heard a discussion about quotas, quality control or how to get more meat on each stem. Quite the contrary. The trees were quietly and systematically drawing up water, channeling it to each and every branch, and assimilating the nutrients it carried. The fruit, then, came naturally and in abundance.

WHAT A PROCESS!

The good news is that we Christians can experience similar inner workings. It all starts with a discipline to open the "seed" of God's Word regularly and to assimilate what we are reading. The Holy Spirit, then, takes what we have assimilated and turns it into spiritual roots. What these roots tap into is the resurrected power of Jesus Christ—a power that has been just waiting to shoot up into the branches.

"By the refreshing and reviving flow of the Holy Spirit through (the abiding life)," says V. Raymond Edman, "there is prayer that prevails, preaching that is powerful, love that is contagious, joy that overflows, and peace that passes understanding."[3] That is beautiful fruit.

"Why is this fruit called the fruit of the Spirit and not the fruit of the Christian?" you may ask.

Probably because the Christian is not the one who produces it. In fact, the Christian *cannot* produce it. Only the Holy Spirit can produce it. It is *His* fruit.

According to R. C. Sproul, it can be recognized as such by its unusual characteristics. It is "uncommon and extraordinary," he says. To show what he means, he selects one particular fruit of the Spirit:

LOVE

"It is the difference," Sproul continues, "between a love that is common and a love that is uncommon, between ordinary love and extraordinary love, between natural love and supernatural love."[4]

It all begins with the love of God, which the Holy Spirit channels through the cross of Christ and pours into our hearts. From there it flows outward as Christlike sensitivity. In those whose lives it transforms, it produces a love for the Lord, a love for God's Word, a love for God's people and a love for the lost—all supernatural. In short, it is God's love in motion using Christians as its channel—something quite different from the love we humans generate ourselves.

Listen to F. B. Meyer describe it:

> To feel toward enemies what others feel toward friends; to descend as rain and sunbeams on the just as well as the unjust; to minister to those who are unprepossessing and repellent as others minister to the attractive and winsome; to be always the same, not subject to moods or fancies or whims; to suffer long; to take no account of evil; to rejoice with the truth; to bear, believe, hope, and endure all things, never to fail—this is love and such love is the achievement of the Holy Spirit alone.[5]

What is my response to such a challenging description? "O God, produce this love through me!"

JOY

is also a work of God, produced through Christians by His Spirit. Unlike happiness, which people work hard to achieve, joy is not dependent upon circumstances. In fact, joy can be ours even in times of turmoil. According to J. I. Packer, "Christians have, so to speak, larger souls than other people. For grief and joy (like desolation and hope, or pain and peace) can coexist in their lives in a way that non-Christians know nothing about."[6]

Jesus is a good example of this "larger soul," for He showed us it is possible to hate what you are going through and still rejoice in what will come of it. "For the joy that was set before [Jesus] endured the cross, despising the shame," the Bible says, "and is set down at the right hand of the throne of God." The anticipation of hearing His Father say "Well done" breathed joyful significance into His earthly pain and joyful purpose into His unspeakable humiliation.

If you conclude that the joy that beckoned to Jesus from heaven must have had real substance to it, you would be right. Holy Spirit-produced joy is very substantive and, because of that, can be marvelously motivating. Jesus knew this joy well. He had experienced it in eternity past before He ever stepped into our world of pain. He couldn't wait to experience it again.

We humans can't even imagine what such unadulterated joy must be like, so the Holy Spirit whets our appetites. "No eye has seen, no ear has heard, no mind has conceived what God has prepared for those who love him," He promises.

Then, in describing the redeemed entering the presence of the Lord, He says, "everlasting joy will crown their heads. Gladness and joy will overtake them."[7] It is this hope that motivates us to persevere. We can taste heaven's joy now, but in the future we will be feasting on it. I don't know about you, but I can hardly wait.

PEACE

is that elusive state of mind we try to achieve whenever we are troubled. We tell ourselves, "Stop being anxious! Calm down!" Unfortunately, such admonitions often fall on deaf ears (ours), and we end up being more nervous than ever.

What is our problem? We are forgetting that peace cannot be worked up. Peace is a gift from God. Right before Jesus left His disciples to go to the cross, He said, "Peace I leave with you; my peace I give you." For those who choose to receive this peace, inner battles have ended. The white flag of surrender is lifted, and a truce is signed and sealed.

Who makes it all possible? God's Holy Spirit.

How does He do it? He goes back in time to the Savior's finished work on the cross—to the place where "he put to death their hostility." Then He applies to our lives the peace the cross accomplished. We in turn appropriate it by turning our personal conflicts over to the Savior. His peace, then, comes into our souls like a flood.

> Peace is...fruit that has the ability
> to calm a troubled soul.

Throughout the ages, writers have described creatively the peace God's Spirit can bring. A hymn writer talked of it as "a river glorious." The author of Proverbs said, "A heart at peace gives life to the body." And "[Christ] himself is our peace," the apostle Paul declared, implying that once we receive Christ's Spirit, we have access to all that Christ is and will continue to be.[8]

In whatever way peace is described, one thing is certain: it is fruit that has the ability to calm a troubled soul. That makes it highly prized.

THE OTHER FRUIT OF THE SPIRIT

is a Christian's portion as well. Take LONGSUFFERING. This fruit is also referred to as "patience." We see it in the life of Jesus Christ. The cross is something He "endured," the writer of Hebrews tells us, selecting a word that suggests a difficult wait.

If the Helper can produce in Jesus an ability to wait patiently, He can produce it in us as well. However, it requires of us the same discipline it required of the Savior. We must focus on future joy rather than on present pain. We must understand that longsuffering, by its very nature, comes only through suffering. That makes it another very precious fruit—and well worth pursuing.

GENTLENESS: The Bible says Jesus "took the children in his arms, put his hands on them and blessed them." His Spirit wants to offer through us a loving touch to others, too, not only to children, but also to the elderly and to those who are physically, emotionally or mentally challenged. He wants us to be a blessing to people of all ages and all conditions.

GOODNESS means living a life without deceit. The Bible makes the necessity of this fruit clear when it stresses what the Lord requires of us. It is "to act justly and to love mercy and to walk humbly with your God." In other words, we are to be known as good, upright people. It is a simple, but basic, Christian requirement.

Associate FAITHFULNESS with trustworthiness. Take a moment each day just to reflect on how trustworthy God is. As a reminder, I suggest reciting the following Scripture verses: "Because of the Lord's great love we are not consumed, for his compassions never fail. They are new every morning; great is your faithfulness."

> Nothing restricts the Spirit's workings more than unconfessed sin....It is up to us, the "branches," to stay pure in body as well as in soul.

Oh, to watch the Spirit produce that kind of faithfulness through us— to keep us true to our marriage vows, true to our business contracts, true to our promise to keep a confidence and true to the multitude of other commitments we have made! "Do it through us, Holy Spirit," we find ourselves pleading, "for we cannot do it on our own."

MEEKNESS is akin to humility. To prepare ourselves for this fruit, it helps to meditate on Christ's condescension from heaven to earth and subsequent life in our midst. It was a life of power contained. The Bible says, "[he] made himself nothing, taking the very nature of a servant." This willingness to go through humiliation is a model for what the Spirit wants to produce in you and me—and can—if we let Him.

SELF-CONTROL is a companion to meekness. It, too, involves restraint—the kind that enabled Jesus to refrain from retaliating, "When they hurled their insults at him."9

Do you ever wish you had more control over your emotions? In and of ourselves, of course, we don't, but the Holy Spirit does—and can impart that control to us. He does not limit Himself to producing fruit selectively. He intends to produce all His fruit in all His followers.

Granted, some followers will evidence more of certain kinds of fruit than others will; but all followers will manifest a sampling of everything. Aren't you glad? Aren't you eager to see what pops out on your branch next? For anything at all to happen, though, we have to fulfill...

OUR DUTIES AS FRUIT BEARERS

1. *Be open to receive.* Just as fruit trees open themselves to receive water, so we Christians must open ourselves to what the Lord wants to do through us. "Be still, and know that I am God," He admonishes. In other words, "Stop trying to produce My fruit on your own. Relax. Expect it to happen. Then when you feel My power coming, let it surge through you." Can you think of anything more exciting than being connected to Jesus the Christ through His Spirit and feeling Him at work in your life?

2. *Keep all passageways clean.* In fruit trees, obstructions hinder the flow of water. In the Christian life, the same thing is true. Nothing restricts the Spirit's workings more than unconfessed sin. Perhaps that is why the Bible says, "If we confess our sins, [God's Son] is faithful and just and will forgive us our sins and purify us from all unrighteousness." It is up to us, the "branches," to stay pure in body as well as in soul.

3. *Soak up nourishment.* Like trees on riverbanks, we Christians have been planted near "streams of living water," but it is our choice whether or not we absorb what the Stream has to offer. "Remain in me,"[10] the Lord commands. This is like saying, "Stay in My Word and make sure My Word stays in you. Talk to Me and listen for My response continually. In other words, draw upon My resources all your waking hours." For those who choose to obey the Lord's command, not enough baskets will be available to gather up all their fruit.

4. *Persevere.* Sometimes fruit is slow in coming. The Holy Spirit has a different timetable for each and every Christian. "When we are expecting the torrent to pour into and fill the well," F. B. Meyer warns, "He fills it by single drops." Then, addressing the temptation to compare ourselves with Christians who bloom early, Meyer adds, "But the results will always be the same—great boldness in witness-bearing, much liberty in

prayer and praise, great grace and beauty in character, self-denying love for those in need, great power through union with the Lord."[11] Yes, some of us may be late bloomers, but it is worth waiting for the results.

5.   *Submit to pruning.* If trees could talk, pruning time would be a likely occasion for them to exercise their vocal cords. The sight of their caretaker coming toward them, shears in hand, would be terrifying. Hear their cry: "No! Don't hurt me, please!" Yet the caretaker keeps right on coming. Why? Because he knows that pruning produces better fruit.

It does in Christians, too. As distasteful as it is to be cut down, cut back or cut off, the hurts of life do make us strong. In fact, it is almost impossible to exhibit great spiritual strength without some kind of suffering. Pain, according to the apostle Peter, proves our faith to be "genuine."[12]

> Everything the Holy Spirit produces through us, He produces not only for our personal benefit, but also for the good of those around us.

One thing we have to remember, though, is that everything the Holy Spirit produces through us, He produces not only for our personal benefit, but also for the good of those around us. The fruit that identifies us as Christians is meant to be offered as...

FOOD FOR HUNGRY SOULS

The trees described in Ezekiel's vision are unusual. Instead of producing fruit during one season only, they produce all year long. They produce summer fruit and winter fruit, autumn fruit and spring fruit. In fact, there is never a time when fruit is not appearing on their branches somewhere. The message seems to be that someone who is spiritually hungry should never go away unfed from spending time with a Christian friend.

Knowing this, we should not be surprised when we learn that the gospel can be tailored to meet the needs of anybody, regardless of age or spirituality. For spiritual "babies," it can be pureed; while for the more mature, it can be served "whole." For those who like a challenge, it can be offered keeping the "shell" intact. Those of us presenting the fruit must be prepared to meet all these challenges. The Holy Spirit is ready to make sure we are.

In God's economy, nothing is wasted. We are reminded of this when we revisit Ezekiel's vision of the heavenly river lined with trees. In that vision even the leaves have a purpose. According to the prophet, they possess...

HEALING PROPERTIES

The analogy is not hard to apply. As we move about in the Spirit, we meet all kinds of people. Many are hurting. Their ailments run the gamut—from physical to mental to emotional to spiritual. As Christians, we can apply Ezekiel's "leaves" to wounds, but we are not able to bring about the healing. However, we can create situations in which the Holy Spirit can.

In the New Testament, creativity in paving the way for miracles abounds. In one case, friends of a paralytic removed tiles from the roof of a house where Jesus was teaching and lowered the sick man through the ceiling. Jesus then gave a command and the man "stood up in front of them, took what he had been lying on and went home praising God."

Another time a centurion asked Jesus to heal his paralyzed servant, and Jesus answered, "'It will be done just as you believed it would.'" Then the Bible records, "And his servant was healed at that very hour."

James, in his Epistle to Jewish believers, instructs anyone who is sick to "call the elders of the church to pray over him and anoint him with oil in the name of the Lord." Then he adds, "And the prayer offered in faith will make the sick person well; the Lord will raise him up."[13] In all these cases, it is the Holy Spirit who does the healing, but it is the Christian who creates the situation in which the Spirit can work.

"What a thrilling study!" you say as you turn to your mentor, who is still beside you under the pear tree. "It is filled with hope. I've learned that the fruit I long to have will be mine if I but yield to the Spirit's power. I'm grateful for that, but I have a question. Can the healing leaves of Ezekiel's vision apply to broken relationships? In other words, can a person get rid of a bitter spirit?"

"Sure can," your teacher answers as he offers you another pear, "but I'll let you search the answer for yourself by having you step into the author's shoes."

Notes

1. Galatians 5:22,23—a combination of versions.
2. Andrew Murray, *Abide in Christ* (Fort Washington, Pa.: Christian Literature Crusade, 1968), p. 101.
3. V. Raymond Edman, *They Found the Secret* (Grand Rapids: Zondervan Publishing House, 1960), p. 98.
4. R. C. Sproul, *The Mystery of the Holy Spirit* (Wheaton, Ill: Tyndale House Publishers, 1990), p. 167.
5. F. B. Meyer, *Daily Meditations* (Dallas, Tex.: Word Books, 1979), September 30.
6. J. I. Packer, *Hot Tub Religion* (Wheaton, Ill.: Tyndale House, 1987), p. 139.
7. The Scripture verses cited in the section "Joy" are as follows: Hebrews 12:2 *(KJV)*; 1 Corinthians 2:9; Isaiah 35:10.
8. The Scripture verses cited in the section "Peace" are as follows: John 14:27; Ephesians 2:16; Proverbs 14:30; Ephesians 2:14.
9. The Scripture verses cited in the section "The Other Fruit of the Spirit" are as follows: Mark 10:16; Micah 6:8; Lamentations 3:22,23; Philippians 2:7; 1 Peter 2:23.
10. The Scripture verses cited in the section "Our Duties As Fruit Bearers" are as follows: Psalm 46:10; 1 John 1:9; John 7:38; 15:4.
11. Meyer, *Daily Meditations*, September 11.
12. First Peter 1:7.
13. The incidents cited in the section "Healing Properties" are based on the following Scripture passages: Luke 5:15-26; Matthew 8:5-13; James 5:14,15.

No More Bitterness

Does a fountain send out from the same
opening both fresh water and bitter water?
JAMES 3:11 *(NASB)*

You are sitting on the bank of the river beside your teacher. You are ready for your next lesson. He asks you to picture yourself sitting at the author's kitchen table, to allow yourself to step into her shoes. You do. You notice a pen in your hand and an open Bible and sheet of paper in front of you. The paper is blank—as blank as it was when you started this project three hours ago. You have been searching for a practical definition of forgiveness, and you have come up short.

Awhile ago you received a call from the Protestant Women of The Chapel in Fort Knox, Kentucky. The chairwoman asked you to fly down in the fall and address her group about the subject of forgiveness. You accepted the invitation.

The minute you hung up, you ran to your desk to see if you had addressed this topic in the past. You discovered you had. Twice. However, the thrust of both lectures was God's forgiveness of sinners. You could find no material at all about how to forgive one another.

I have a challenging search ahead of me, you conclude, as you pull back from the table. Then you remember the pool in your backyard. Soon school will be out for the summer, and friends will be coming over to swim. Maybe you can use them as resource persons.

Unfortunately, your poolside interviews prove to be as frustrating as your personal search. One friend says, "You know, Peg, I've been a Christian a long time, but for the life of me, I can't put into words what it means to forgive somebody."

Another says, "To forgive means to pardon."

"But what do you actually *do* when you pardon somebody?" you ask. She shrugs.

I guess I'm starting in the wrong place, you think. *Maybe if I research bitterness, I'll be able to come up with a definition of forgiveness. I'll draw on personal experience. I remember the time our family lost its savings in a business deal gone sour. "Letting go" of that disaster was difficult. I wanted to get even, to make my husband's business partner pay for his shady dealings.*

SPLASH!

Your thoughts leave the past and return to the present. You are standing by the pool. One of the kids has just dived in. You watch him swim. How clean the water is! It is hard to believe this pool was filthy just a short while ago.

It got polluted when you and your husband were removing the cover. You didn't bother to clean the cover first because you were convinced you could slide it off, debris and all. How wrong you were! You watched in horror as a huge blob of black sludge slid in and started to dissipate. Forward it advanced. Sideways it crept. Soon the whole pool was slate gray, leaves and sticks and even a dead mouse floating on the surface. It took a lot of work to clean up the mess.

As you stand there gazing into the water, now pure, you realize a spiritual application can be drawn from this. The human heart can get just as contaminated as the pool—if we choose to let it. Opportunities abound. Every time we are lied to, stolen from, slandered, betrayed or abused, we choose how we are going to react. Will we bury the past, realizing we can't change it anyway? Or will we choose to revisit it regularly, allowing its powerful pollutants to contaminate our lives?

We face the same choice whenever we become victims of an accident, suffer a disability, are financially stressed, endure a prolonged illness or mourn the death of a loved one. Any one of these reversals is capable of giving us a negative orientation—an orientation that can easily control us.

You remember the Bible saying, "Be careful that none of you fails to respond to the grace which God gives, for if he does there can very easily spring up in him a bitter spirit which is not only bad in itself but can also poison the lives of many others."[1] Unfortunately, among these "many others" are people dear to us—people we love and don't want to hurt. Yet they unwittingly become the targets of our frustration.

Some of us go as far as to vent our frustration on targets outside, as well as inside, our family circles. When we do, we risk alienating everybody who knows us, including the Lord. In the future, we may try to pray, but words won't come. We may open the Bible, but we won't be able to concentrate on what we are reading. Bitterness will have consumed us.

"If you do not forgive men their sins," the Bible says, "your Father will not forgive your sins."[2] These words are unnerving. To get to their meaning, you review what you know about God's plan of redemption, which, the Bible assures, is carried out regardless of human shortcomings. According to God's Word, our salvation is not dependent upon our forgiveness of others. You know that. On the other hand, if we do not forgive others, we can not really participate in the blessings of God's forgiveness of us. We are in bondage to our own resentful spirits. Only when we let God's pardon continue its flow right on through us are we set free.

This illumination makes you realize you are making progress in your study. You need to learn more, though—much more. Suddenly you remember that you and your husband, Lee, are team teaching a Bible class of about 180 adults. *Why don't we turn this topic of forgiveness over to them?* you think. *There are some really sharp minds in that group. Maybe together we can formulate a definition.* So that is what you do. The next Sunday morning you ask the class,

WHAT IS FORGIVENESS?

The following thoughts are forthcoming:
  • *Forgiveness is a product of God's grace.* "We humans cannot erase our hurts by ourselves," a class member observes. "The 'incident,' what-

ever it happens to be, keeps replaying in our heads. We have been wronged, and we want revenge. If there's going to be a change of attitude, God is going to have to bring it about."

• *Forgiveness requires human action.* "Christians must offer their bodies as channels for the Holy Spirit to move through," another member contributes. "To make an apology, the Spirit needs a human mouth. To write a note or to pick up a phone, He needs a human hand. To take a step toward reconciliation, He needs two human feet. 'If you are offering your gift at the altar,' the Bible says, 'and there remember that your brother has something against you, leave your gift there in front of the altar. First go and be reconciled to your brother; then come and offer your gift.'"[3]

> God faces the fact that a chasm is separating the offender from Himself, and He takes the initiative to bring about reconciliation.

• *Forgiveness demands disposing of personal debris.* "In other words," someone explains, "haul a wheelbarrow up to your heart and toss in all your secret junk. Do not hold a garage sale. Instead, take every grievance you have, put it into a container, seal it and mark it HAZARDOUS WASTE: DO NOT OPEN. When that's done, bury the container. Then erect a sign that says, NO DIGGING ALLOWED!"

You realize this student has just described what the Lord does with the offenses we commit against Him—offenses He calls "sins." He buries them—and shovel still in hand, promises, "'[Your] sins and lawless acts I will remember no more.'"[4] It is not that God "forgets" them. They sent His Son to the cross. Rather, He chooses not to dig them up. The class finds this aspect of forgiveness fascinating. So do you.

Your husband, Lee, points out more intriguing insights: God doesn't excuse our wrongdoing (*Well, he/she is only human.*). Nor does He smooth things over (*What happened is not THAT bad!*). He certainly doesn't act as if there is no breach of fellowship (*Everything between us is fine.*). Rather, God faces the fact that a chasm is separating the offender from Himself, and He takes the initiative to bring about reconciliation. What a role model for human forgiveness!

• *Forgiveness is surrendering the right to retaliate.* "If this is not done," a participant insists, "the heart will only be further contaminated. For we humans are quite creative in coming up with ways to make a person 'pay.' For example, we may refuse to discuss the situation; this is known as 'the silent treatment.' Or we may release a barrage of hurtful words. Or we may deliberately embarrass the offender in the presence of others. It is easy to become a slave to any one of these practices. However, there is a way out. Once we release the offender from paying his 'debt,' we will find that we have released ourselves as well."

You ask the class to turn to the Gospel of Matthew, chapter 18. You read the story of three people involved in the process of forgiveness. You designate them A, B and C. You relate how A forgives B a huge amount of money, but B refuses to forgive C a mere pittance. Who ends up in prison? C does—because he cannot pay B. Interestingly enough, B also ends up incarcerated. He is turned over to the jailers "to be tortured," the Bible says.[5] Why? Because B refuses to let A's forgiveness continue its flow through him into C's life. As a result, B will spend his life in a bondage of his own making—unless, of course, he decides to forgive C's debt.

> Forgiveness means bearing,
> without malice, the consequences
> of the offender's actions.

The class has done an excellent job. This last insight helps you feel ready to present your material to the women on the military base, but you come to that conclusion too hastily. In the providence of God, a dear friend, Pastor Stanley Rockafellow, comes to spend the night in your home. In the course of conversation, the subject of forgiveness surfaces. You decide to try your newly formed definition on this astute Bible teacher. Stanley listens intently. When you are finished, he says, "It's a great definition, Peg,—as far as it goes."

"What do you mean, 'as far as it goes'"?

"Well, to make the definition complete," Stanley answers, "you need to add these words:

• *Forgiveness means bearing, without malice, the consequences of the offender's actions."*

"Bearing the consequences of the offender's action!"

"Well, that's what Jesus did," Stanley reminds you. "Not only did He pay the debt of our sin by dying in our place, but He also bore the consequences of that sin by suffering the hell we deserve."

"How does that translate horizontally?" you ask.

"It translates into a willingness to endure whatever the consequences of the broken relationship are, whether they be stares, whispers, backbiting, public humiliation, a spurning of your attempt at reconciliation, even a mocking of that attempt, making you look foolish. That can be 'hell.'"

"I can't forgive like that!" you exclaim. "Nobody can!"

WHAT DO I DO IF I CAN'T FORGIVE?

The Kentucky engagement is now only a few days away. You realize you are stymied. You cannot address this issue of forgiveness without an answer to the question you just formed. So you send up a plea for help. You are trusting God's Spirit to honor your request, but you are wondering how He will do it. Probably through the pastor's sermon, you surmise. So you go to church that Sunday morning with open ears. You are disappointed. The pastor doesn't even mention forgiveness. Oh well, you still have the evening service. That night you are equally alert, but you come home disappointed again. You slump into an easy chair. Now what?

Next to the chair is a stack of books a friend had given you that morning. "Peg," the elderly woman had said, "I know I'm not going to live much longer, and I don't want to leave these texts from my Bible school days to my pagan kids. Would you like to have them?"

"I would *love* to have them," you had assured this special saint. "And I will use them. Thank you!"

You are gazing now upon that stack of books. You decide to pick up the top one. *Let me see what this is about,* you think. You open it at random. You look at the words on the page. Suddenly you see it. In letters that seem to be a foot high, a Scripture verse leaps out. It provides the answer to your question. Unbelievable! Quickly you open your Bible so you can read the verse in its context.

The passage is taken from the fifteenth chapter of the book of Exodus. Moses is leading the Israelites through the desert. For the last three days they have found no water. When the group arrives at Marah, they find an oasis, but the water is not drinkable. It is "bitter," the Bible says. Frantic, the people start venting their frustration on Moses. He is not the cause of the problem, but that doesn't seem to matter. He is blamed anyway.

> The cure is in a tree. The tree. The tree on which Jesus died. There's power in that tree! Sinners can be reconciled to God; and sinners can be reconciled to each other.

Helpless, Moses cries out to the Lord. The Lord answers by showing him a tree. Moses, then, throws a branch of that tree into the water. Miraculously, the water becomes pure.[6]

Your heart leaps into your throat. You see it clearly. The cure is in a tree. *The* tree. The tree on which Jesus died. There's power in that tree! Sinners can be reconciled to God; and sinners can be reconciled to each other. For the latter to take place, though, we, who can't forgive, must "throw the tree" into our bitter situations. In other words, we must do what we can and let God do what we can't.

You remember the story of Corrie ten Boom, whose family provided a hiding place for persecuted Jews during World War II. Unfortunately, the clandestine activities were discovered, and the family members were sent to concentration camps. Corrie survived. After the war, while on a lecture tour in Munich, she met a guard from Ravensbruck. He had since become a Christian. When he extended his hand in reconciliation, Corrie recoiled. Instead of being filled with forgiveness, she was flooded with memories of the atrocities her family had endured. Bitterness was gripping her soul.

"Jesus, help me!" she cried. "I can extend my hand, but you must supply the feeling."

Immediately, Corrie says, a current of warmth started to course through her body. It enabled her to look the guard in the eye and say, "I forgive you, brother, with my whole heart."

What a testimony to the power of the tree! What a testimony to Corrie, who symbolically grabbed that tree and flung a branch into her bitterness, demonstrating "it is not on our forgiveness...that the world's healing hinges, but on His."[7]

LEE, COME HERE!

You are so excited about discovering this answer to your question—and just in the nick of time—you immediately call out to your husband, who is in another room. He comes running.

"Do you know what you're supposed to do when you can't forgive somebody?" you ask. "You're supposed to 'throw in the tree!'"

"I thought you were supposed to throw in the towel," he laughs.

"That's giving up," you reply. "Throwing in the tree is giving over."

Then you recount Moses' story, ending with the tossing of the branch into the water and its miraculous result. Lee is quiet for a moment as he ponders the story's implications. Then he responds, "It seems to me, Peg, that when you throw in the tree, you have to climb upon it."

You feel as if you have just been stabbed. You know exactly what he means. You have to "die"—"die" to what you would like to see happen to the offender. On that tree is a place for every part of your body to be sacrificed: for your thoughts (will I think positively or negatively?); for your eyes (will I see the offender as God does?); for your ears (will I filter out the nasty things that are said?); for your mouth (will I speak the truth in love?); for your heart (will I harbor bitterness or forgiveness?); for your hands (will I determine to reach out in compassion?); for your knees (will I pray for this one who is despitefully using me?); and for your feet (will I take that first step toward reconciliation?).

You are forced to face the fact that you may do all these things without experiencing the restoration of your broken relationship. Restoration takes two. You also realize the offender may continue to "crucify" you daily, nailing you painfully to that tree.

"How long do I have to stay on the Cross?" you will cry.

"Until you are dead," will be the Spirit's reply.

"How will I know when I'm dead?"

"When it doesn't hurt anymore," He will answer. Then He may add, "but don't get discouraged. You HAVE to 'die' in order to live. Remember? Death is your route to..."

RESURRECTION POWER!

Whether or not a broken relationship is ever mended, you now know you can be spiritually free. You can advance in your Christian walk, wiser for what you have learned. You no longer need to seek revenge. "It is mine to avenge," God says, "I will repay."

As for your personal responsibilities, "If your enemy is hungry, feed him; if he is thirsty, give him something to drink," you are reminded. "Do not be overcome by evil, but overcome evil with good."

Who knows? Perhaps by your "good behavior in Christ," your offender will "be ashamed" and return to the "Shepherd and Overseer of [his] soul," asking for God's forgiveness.[8]

ON TO KENTUCKY

You do board the plane for Fort Knox. You do give your lectures about forgiveness. Many more seminars follow as a result. As you continue to bone up on this fascinating subject, you discover that others before you searched for the answers, too, and some of them were led to the same Scripture passages you were. Listen to these words from Amy Carmichael: "If thou must pass through Marah, fear not, for He will show thee a Tree, which when thou shalt cast it into the waters, shall make the bitter waters sweet."[9] Amazing!

An epilogue to Moses' experience at Marah intrigues you. After the Israelites left there, "they came to Elim," the Bible says, "where there were twelve springs and seventy palm trees, and they camped there near the water."[10]

Stepping out of the author's shoes, you turn to your teacher, who is still beside you on the riverbank. "Oh, to camp by the waters of forgiveness for the rest of my natural life," you say. "To be rid of bitterness forever. That is my desire."

"Mine too," he replies. "Staying close to the water is the secret to experiencing that abundant life. But before I leave you, I have one more lesson to teach you. Not only can the Spirit heal bitter spirits, He can heal broken bodies as well. Allow yourself to become the author again and experience an eye-popping miracle."

Notes

1. Hebrews 12:15 *(Phillips)*.
2. Matthew 6:15.
3. Matthew 5:23,24.
4. Hebrews 10:17.
5. This story is based on Matthew 18:21-35.
6. This account is based on Exodus 15:22-25.
7. Corrie ten Boom with John and Elizabeth Sherrill, *The Hiding Place* (Grand Rapids: Chosen Books, 1971), p. 215.
8. The section "Resurrection Power!" is based on the following Scripture verses: Romans 12:20,21; 1 Peter 3:16; 1 Peter 2:19-25.
9. Amy Carmichael, *His Thoughts Said, His Father Said* (Fort Washington, Pa.: Christian Literature Crusade, n.d.), p. 6.
10. Exodus 15:27.

A Healing Touch

[By the pool of Bethesda] a great number of disabled
people used to lie—the blind, the lame, the paralyzed—
and they waited for the moving of the waters.*

JOHN 5:3

You are on the bank of the river beside your mentor. Together you are watching the water splash upon the sand, and together you are marveling at its benefits.

"I want to introduce you to another benefit the water has," your teacher says. "I want you to understand its healing properties. In order to accomplish this, I invite you to step again into the author's shoes. Only this time picture yourself sitting at a desk, about to open an annual Christmas letter from her (your) oldest son, Dirk, and his wife, Laurie."

In your mind you successfully make the transition your guide is requesting. You picture yourself at the author's desk, slitting the envelope to her son's letter. You notice the paper inside is a festive green. You remove it and unfold it. Your eyes fall on the title, "The Year of Mark." Your mind jumps backward 10 months.

It is late at night. The phone jars you awake. Your husband, Lee, picks

*This last clause is not included in all manuscripts.

it up. His voice shows concern. After just a few minutes he hangs up and gives you the news: "Little Mark is in the Pediatric Intensive Care Unit (PICU) of Sinai Hospital in Baltimore. He was admitted in critical condition. His blood chemistry is life threatening, and the cause is unknown. He is also quite low on blood, so transfusions are under way in an attempt to stabilize him. Let's pray."

You both sigh, and together you do pray for Mark, your grandson of 20 months. As your requests rise to heaven, you feel your heartbeat quicken. Mark's symptoms sound serious enough in and of themselves, yet something tells you the root problem may be even worse—perhaps fatal. You are seized with a feeling of helplessness.

It is impossible to go back to sleep. You toss, you turn, and throughout the remaining hours of darkness, you cry out to your heavenly Father. Suddenly you are aware that you are not alone. Your Helper is there, right beside you in the room, and He is speaking. Although His voice is inaudible, it is so clear that you know exactly what He is saying. He is commissioning you to become an intercessor—an intercessor with no holds barred.

This kind of intercession, you realize, is what Jesus entered into in the Garden of Gethsemane. As He prostrated Himself beneath the olive branches, "His sweat was like drops of blood falling to the ground."[1] He was about to accomplish our redemption by dying the death we deserved, and His cries of agony were piercing the heavy air.

As you are lying in the darkness, you feel God's eternal arms slip reassuringly underneath you. You listen patiently for...

THE HOLY SPIRIT'S GENTLE WHISPER

"How much do you love your grandson Mark?"

"With all my heart," you answer.

"So much so that you are willing to place yourself in Mark's stead?"

"What do you mean?"

"Are you willing to die, if necessary, in order that Mark might live?"

You hesitate just a second. "I am willing," you answer.

"Then I can count on you to be an effective intercessor," the whisper confirms, "for the highest order of intercessory prayer takes place when the one who is praying so identifies with the person in need that he or she is willing to take that person's place. Because Jesus took your place on the cross, even to the point of suffering hell for you, His prayers on your behalf are effectual. 'Follow in his steps,'[2] the Bible says."

"I want to," you reply.

As you lie there, your commitment having been made, it is as if the Spirit is embracing you. Is He fortifying you for what lies ahead? Is He sealing your commitment before the Father and His Son, Jesus the Christ? Whatever He is doing, you know it is good.

With the arrival of dawn, you...

SPRING INTO ACTION

The first thing you do is to phone all family members, alerting them to the crisis. Then you start notifying friends—friends you know you can trust. They prove their faithfulness in marvelous ways. Your friend El relates how one night after praying for Mark, she was awakened at dawn by a voice that said, "Trust Me," and her heart quietly answered, "I will."

Joan offers to drive you to Maryland, reminding you that she is a grandmother, too. "A child of your child is twice your child," she says.

> It is comforting to have your prayer partners beside you in the "water."

Cheryl retreats to her yellow prayer chair, then after each session with the Lord phones for the latest medical report. Teddie hugs you on the way into church, weeping at the desperateness of the situation. Terry and Jack, who are in pain regarding their own grandson, sit beside you in the pew. You thank God for these kinds of friends.

Other friends spring into action as well. Your pastor puts a prayer chain into motion. Judy, in Michigan, brings Mark's needs to her Bible study group. Barbara, the chairwoman of an upcoming conference to be held on Hilton Head Island—a speaking engagement you anticipate having to cancel—alerts conference leaders in other states. Soon Mark is being lifted up in areas throughout the country. How blessed you feel! It is as if you have been immersed afresh in God's Spirit and are now floating effortlessly in His love. It is comforting to have your prayer partners beside you in the "water."

Your thoughts come back to the present, to the festive green paper you are holding in your hand. You feel ready now to have more memories surface as you read...

DIRK AND LAURIE'S 1994 CHRISTMAS LETTER

Last year we were joking about Mark not walking yet. This year we discovered the reason why. February 1, Mark was diagnosed as having Systemic Onset Juvenile Rheumatoid Arthritis (Still's disease), the most serious form of JRA that not only affects the joints but the internal organs as well. At that time Mark had arthritis in his neck, shoulders, elbows, wrists, hips, knees, ankles, and toes. He also had an enlarged liver and spleen. This diagnosis put so many puzzle pieces into place, among them the rash and the late walking.

Unknown to everyone at the time, Mark's condition was so advanced that his body would soon be triggered into a self-destructive process that would nearly take his life....

As you read these words, you remember your daughter-in-law Laurie telling you about the several "blood draws" Mark had to endure upon his admission to the hospital. The results were off the charts. Incredulous doctors ordered the nurse to take Mark's blood again and again. When she came with her needle the fourth time, she said, "I'm so sorry, Mark, I have to hurt you." And Mark, not talking yet but wanting to let the nurse know he understood, flung his little arms around her neck and kissed her.

In addition to liver, spleen and brain involvement, Mark's internal condition led to mild heart failure, significant bone marrow, blood, and spinal fluid abnormalities, plus a host of other problems. Mark endured spinal taps, bone marrow aspirations and biopsies, a lymph node biopsy, complete body scans, multiple blood, platelet and human antibody transfusions, and more....

When you finish reading this section, you remember your son Dirk telling you how hard it was to watch Mark's little body being fed through the huge CAT scanner. The Still's diagnosis had been rejected and several malignant conditions were now suspected. How difficult it was, Dirk said, to see "slices" of his son's organs come up on the screen and then to wait as the doctor scrutinized them for tumors.

During this tedious ordeal, Dirk was very conscious that the Holy Spirit was with him. At one point, his eye caught the name of the equipment's manufacturer. It was the company his father worked for, so he knew he had the best scanner in the world—or so he had been led to believe. Anyway, it brought him comfort. At times like these, comfort, whatever its source, is welcome.

By the end of the diagnostic sessions, which included X-ray and nuclear imaging as well as CAT scans, no tumors and no massive invasion of cancer had been found—to the surprise of many involved in the case. Although this was certainly good news to the family, it was at the same time mystifying to the medical team working on Mark. His condition was so severe and his internal state so fragile that there had to be an explanation. What was it?

An intensive search was conducted for three more days to find the root cause of Mark's symptoms. In the end, without unanimity among the physicians, Mark was rediagnosed with a fatal condition called FEL (familial erythrophagocytic lymphohistiocytosis). Prognosis: death in 2 to 24 months. Technical reports that dealt with the symptoms and treatment of FEL were placed at Mark's bedside for Dirk and Laurie's perusal. In the typically dry language of the medical community, the reports characterized FEL as "uniformly rapidly fatal." It was a devastating conclusion—one that offered no hope.

Shortly after receiving this news, you and Lee arrive...

AT THE HOSPITAL

The mood in the PICU is grim. Your eyes are drawn to the little body in the bed to the right. It is Mark. His eyes are shut and his arms are tied to keep him from pulling out the tubes. Fluids are dripping, and monitors are beeping. Mark's fever is high, his organs are failing and his blood is in the process of destroying itself. Laurie is at her son's side. She, too, is conscious of the Spirit's presence.

Because it is shortly after Valentine's Day, Dirk decides to bring Mark's two sisters to see their little brother. So Jessica, six, and Valerie, four, arrive, bearing gifts. By ironing beads together, they have created hearts. You wonder, though, if Mark will be able to appreciate their love offerings, for his eyes have not been tracking, and he is groggy from his medication.

The nurse removes Mark's restraints and sets up two chairs beside Mark's bed. After Laurie explains the strange equipment to Mark's sisters, including the flow of the "yucky" yellow fluid that is Mark's "food," the girls climb up on the chairs. Jessica goes first. Cautiously, she leans over the rail and hands her brother his valentine. You watch as Mark's eyelids flutter and a little arm reaches out, takes the present, and brings it to the front of his nose. Then he repeats the motion with Valerie's valentine. It is an encouraging moment.

Mark's condition, however, continues to deteriorate. When it is time for lunch, the family goes in shifts...

To the Cafeteria

You, Lee and Dirk eat together. You are grateful for this time away from the hustle in the intensive care unit, for you are feeling the need to talk frankly and realistically to your son. After Lee summarizes the situation and offers what he hopes is consolation, you swallow and begin. "Dirk, it's hard for me to ask you this question, but I must. Are you willing to give your son to the Lord?"

Dirk thinks hard. "He's my only son," he says.

You are silent for a moment. Then you venture, "God gave His only Son for you."

"I have wanted to relinquish him," Dirk admits, "but I haven't been able to do it. I know Mark is in bad shape. I don't want him to suffer." Then Dirk pauses. "Do you know what I would miss most, Mom?"

"What?"

"Holding Mark in my lap." Then he says, "Mom, do you think Pop Pop would hold Mark for me?"

Your eyes brim. You are thinking, *Pop Pop is MY father, Dirk's grand-father, Mark's great grandfather—and he went to heaven years ago!* "Pop Pop would *love* to hold Mark for you," you reassure him.

SWISH! With these words, it is as if the curtains of the heavenly throne room are swept back and you are treated to a glimpse of glory. *Why, there he is: Pop Pop! And there's Mother, too! And Jesus! And Mark! Oh Lord, thank You for this marvelous reassurance! I know now that no matter what the outcome, Mark will be cared for! You have shown me that the whole situation is being immersed in Your Spirit's love.*

"Let's pray over Mark," Lee suggests, jolting you back to the need at hand.

Then Dirk adds, "Please pray that whatever God decides to do, He does it quickly, decisively and mercifully."

BACK TO THE
INTENSIVE CARE UNIT

Amid the high-powered activity in that room—activity that is constant—the three of you lay hands on Mark's feverish forehead, and Lee formulates the request. "Heavenly Father," he says, "You are able to raise up this little boy. We know that. And that is certainly our desire. For we love him and want to watch him grow into manhood. However, we acknowledge You as the Sovereign Lord. You see the bigger picture, and You may have a better plan. So we are trusting You to do the best thing, whatever it is. Please, though, whatever You do, be quick, decisive and merciful. In Jesus' name. Amen."

The next day, the elders of the church come, anoint Mark with oil and pray over him. According to Dirk, their prayer is similar. They call upon Jehovah Rapha (the Lord thy Healer) to cure him. But they also express their trust in the Sovereign Lord, relying on Him to do that which is right in His own eyes. Dirk comes away from that prayer session with the feeling that in his hour of need, the Holy Spirit is there, and He is the One doing the *real* praying. As a result of this comforting thought, Dirk and Laurie have peace. Not lack of pain, but peace. They also experience a closeness to God they later say is unlike anything they have ever known.

Within 48 hours...

A Dramatic Change Begins

Mark's blood stops attacking itself and begins the process of rebuilding. His organs stop enlarging and start the long transition back to normal size and function. His fever gradually abates. In a few days Mark is well enough to be released from intensive care. Shortly after that he is released from the hospital altogether to enter a routine outpatient monitoring and treatment mode. The doctors proclaim, "We no longer have any excuse to hold him."

When the scheduled moment of departure comes, doctors and nurses line the corridor and watch Mark walk—on his own power—through the hospital doors. One nurse is convinced that faith is what healed Mark—and says as much. It is a thrilling moment, with credit going to the One who did it all.

Two weeks later Mark is running around your apartment like any normal two-year-old. When his daddy says, "Mark, show us where the Lord healed you," the little boy lifts his T-shirt and points to the scar from his biopsy incision. Then he proudly announces, "Owie!"

Your eyes strain to focus on the conclusion of your son's 1994 Christmas letter:

> Prayers were answered. Mark is a walking miracle. Even the most optimistic outcome projected by any of the doctors and specialists involved with this case has been surpassed by Mark's complete recovery.

As you read these words, you find yourself rejoicing all over again, but you can't help having a certain reserve. For you know that although Mark, who will be six by the time this book is published, looks and acts normal, he still has Juvenile Rheumatoid Arthritis (Still's disease), which, it turns out, was the correct diagnosis after all of the underlying cause of Mark's problem. (Mark's case was so severe that it mimicked FEL, even to the point where, interestingly enough, members of the PICU medical team still refuse to believe the Still's diagnosis.)

The disease is now in medical remission, but Mark's condition has to be monitored regularly. He also requires medication daily. So you have to explain to people that what he was healed from was "the total body rampage" that nearly took his life. He has not yet been healed of Still's disease, which periodically "flares."

As you think about this, you are reminded afresh that God doesn't heal every person who asks. All Christians, however, will ultimately be healed in heaven. Meanwhile, some of us are forced to live with physical or mental problems; others, with disease; and all, with the ravages of the aging process. We are all, in a physical sense, "terminal." This knowledge serves to keep us dependent on the Holy Spirit of God.

As you lay the green paper down on your desk, you thank God for the One He sent to be your Helper in the midst of trials—the One who, when you relinquish what is rightfully His anyway, sometimes allows you to keep it a while longer. How many days comprise the "while longer" is a mystery, so you ask God to help you praise Him no matter what the future holds. The Bible asserts "His way is perfect,"[3] even when it seems imperfect to human eyes. What comfort for those who have lost children or grandchildren!

> In times of trials it is
> absolutely necessary...to
> know God personally!

In times of trials it is absolutely necessary, you realize, to know God personally! To know the Father, who controls all things. To know the Son, who died that we might have eternal life. To know the Spirit, the One who never leaves us nor forsakes us.[4] It is enough to make any Christian want to shout, "Hallelujah!"

<hr/>

So you do. When you are finished proclaiming God's praises, you realize who you are. You are not the author anymore. You are you. You are on the bank of the river beside your beloved Christian teacher, who is looking at you and smiling. "Your lessons for the moment are over," he says. "You have concluded a segment of your schooling in the ways of the Holy Spirit, the 'water.' Now it's time for you to teach someone else what I have taught you. It's time for you yourself to become a mentor."

With these words, he gives you a hug, pauses a moment, then dives back into the river.

You watch until his head pops up. Then you hear him shout, "If you need me, you know where to find me. I'll be either on the bank looking for another pupil or in the water teaching someone to swim."

You watch as he glides away. *There goes my instructor!* you think. *Yet I'm not afraid. I can't believe it! Why, not too long ago I was terrified even to put my foot into the water. Now I expose my whole body to it— and I do so day after day. But am I capable of instructing someone else?*

On my own power, I have to say, I don't think so, I'm not up to it. But I do have a Helper, God's Holy Spirit, who says I can do everything through Christ who gives me strength.[5] I must admit, He has afforded me some wonderful experiences. I have stepped into the shoes of patriarchs, prophets and disciples. I have listened to authors, past and present, share their words of wisdom. I've been given advice on how to let the Spirit cover my walk, my prayer life, my outreach, my desires and my attitudes. I have even received a new heart in the process. That's probably what gave me the courage to plunge into the "water" all the way, letting go of Self, of bitterness and the desire to control my own destiny and the destiny of those I love. In short, it's been an incredible journey, and I wouldn't have missed any part of it.

I know, though, that the victories I'm enjoying today are not necessarily the victories I'll enjoy tomorrow. Each and every day I have to rely afresh on the Spirit. Maybe that's the biggest learning experience of all. So perhaps I AM ready to instruct someone else. There's only one way to find out.

SPLASH! You are back in the water.

How refreshing it feels! How enfolding! How empowering! How energizing! *I was on the bank too long,* you think. *Now I'm back where I belong, there's no question about it. At last I have a spiritual home. It's the river. Now I want to open that "home" to others.*

Notes

1. Luke 22:44.
2. First Peter 2:21.
3. Psalm 18:30.
4. See Hebrews 13:5.
5. See Philippians 4:13.

Epilogue

~~~~~~~~

You find yourself swimming in the deep part of the river. Suddenly you notice someone standing on the beach. He is dressed in shorts, a top and sandals, just as you were not long ago. He looks as if he is fascinated by the water and may even desire to step into it, but for some reason he seems afraid.

You swim toward the beach. When you reach shallow waters, you stand up. Then you splash your way toward the spectator.

"Come on in," you invite in a tone reminiscent of the one your guide used when addressing you. "The water's great."

"No thanks," he answers. "I can't swim."

"No problem," you counter. "I'll teach you."

"I'm not sure I want to learn," he protests.

"That's too bad," you comment. "You're missing a thrill."

"That's what I've heard."

"Then why don't you try it?" You point to a spot in the shallows. "Here. Take off your sandals and step in right here."

He obeys, cautiously touching his toes to the wetness.

He draws back quickly. "It's cold."

"It does seem that way at first," you assure him, "but the longer you are in it, the more accustomed you will become. Try again."

He does, letting the water cover his feet. He looks pleased.

You move backward a few steps, the way your teacher did with you. Then you beckon again. "Let the water cover your knees."

Hesitantly he moves forward. You smile. "Slowly now," you advise. Then you urge, "Keep coming." Meanwhile, you continue to back up.

"Move farther out," you shout from the deep part. "You'll like the feel of the current." Soon he is submerged up to the waist. Pressing against the weight of the water is quite a struggle now. He is obviously having trouble keeping his feet on the bottom. You also notice with delight that with each and every step more and more of him is disappearing.

By now you are treading water. As you are continuing to maneuver backward, he is advancing. Eventually he progresses up to his neck.

"This is as far as I go," he announces, as the water touches his ears. You can't help smiling as you remember your own reluctance at this point.

"Don't stop now," you encourage. "Continue to come."

"I can't," he tries to explain. "I will drown."

"No, you won't," you reassure him. "You will learn to swim. But to do so, you must let the water cover your head. Don't worry about the consequences. I'm here. I won't let anything bad happen."

You realize he is evaluating whether or not he can trust you. He must have decided he can, for suddenly he shouts, "Here goes nothing!" Then he shuts his eyes, holds his nose and goes under. *He committed a lot faster than I did,* you think.

He thrashes around like a madman. Then his head breaks the surface. You are right beside him, supporting him from underneath with your hand.

"Give up the struggle," you advise. "Let the water support you. It will— if you just give it a chance."

You know he is going through an exercise in mental discipline, but he appears to be winning the battle. "Hey, I'm floating," he informs you.

"I know," you smile, gradually withdrawing support. "The water is holding you up. Before long you'll be swimming—then diving—and bringing up treasure with the best of them."

In your heart you know that even more blessings are in store for your pupil, just as they were in store for you. Soon he will find himself in the middle of somebody's desert, offering a cup of cold water in the Savior's name. He will be transported to fishing areas, where he can "catch" a few souls. He will even take a rest on the banks, alongside of you and *your* mentor, and together you will savor some fruit of the Spirit. You can hardly wait.

It will be exciting to introduce people to all the river has to offer, you think. *The very thought of it makes me grateful all over again for my* guide. Oh, how I want to be to others what he was to me! Oh, how I want to help them know the Holy Spirit of God in an ever-deeper, ever-more-intimate way! I want them to be satisfied and yet to be still thirsty, for that's the fascinating paradox of what it means to be a Christian—a Christian who has stepped into the water, has learned how to "swim," has even explored the depths, yet knows when it's time to relax and go with the flow, trusting for the "more" that always lies ahead.

Study Guide

CHAPTER 1: PARCHED GROUND

1. Describe a time when you yearned for water (either for a drink or for rain). What makes water precious? What life situations drive us to become thirsty for God? What changes occur when the Holy Spirit refreshes a soul?

2. Do you agree with John MacArthur's statement that "The tragedy in so many Christian lives is not the tragedy of living horribly immoral lives, it's the tragedy of living disastrously inconsequential lives"? Why or why not? Do you think the Church today is more or less in need of a Holy Spirit revival than it was in times past? Explain.

3. Read Matthew 16:18 and Ephesians 1:22,23; 3:10,11. What promises are made concerning the Church? For the Church to reach its full potential, what must happen first (see Acts 3:19)?

4. How would you explain to a professing but not necessarily "possessing" Christian what is meant by the "living water" Jesus came to give (John 4:10)?

CHAPTER 2: MEETING THE HELPER

1. What images come to mind when you think of the Holy Spirit? In what ways is He obscure?

2. What questions about the Holy Spirit would you like to ask God the Father? God the Son? God the Holy Spirit Himself?

3. Read the following Scripture verses, listing the Spirit's functions: Genesis 1:2; Job 33:4; Psalm 139:7-10; John 15:26; 16:6,13,14; Romans 8:2,11,15,16,26,27; 1 Corinthians 2:9-16; Ephesians 1:13,14; 2 Thessalonians

2:13; 2 Peter 1:20,21. Which of these functions is most dear to you at this stage of your spiritual growth? Why?

4. What does Thomas Arnold mean when he says, "He who does not know God the Holy Spirit cannot know God at all"?

CHAPTER 3: CLOUDBURSTS OF BLESSING

1. Describe a time when you got caught in a cloudburst and didn't like it. When you got drenched and loved it. What made the difference? Relate your answer to the outpouring of spiritual blessings.
2. Restate (without using words that relate to water) the promises God makes in Isaiah 41:17,18; 44:3,4; 49:10; John 4:14; 7:37,38; Revelation 21:6.
3. What did God mean when He said in Jeremiah 2:13, "My people...have dug their own cisterns, broken cisterns that cannot hold water"? In what ways is that statement true in our generation?
4. Share a time when you felt acutely aware of the Holy Spirit's presence. Why do you think you were more aware of Him then than at other times? What can you do to pave the way for a more continuous awareness of His presence?

CHAPTER 4: A REASON TO FEAR

1. Give an example of a time when you failed to heed a warning and were later sorry. Why are we reluctant to pay attention to warnings? When is it wise to take risks? When foolhardy?
2. What warning is given in Exodus 20:4? What made the Israelites disobey this warning (see Exod. 32)? How did Moses react to their disobedience? How did Aaron react to Moses' reprimand? What price did the people pay for their disobedience? Why do you think the price was so high?
3. What does Elihu mean by the statement, "[God] brings the clouds to punish men, or to water his earth and show his love" (Job 37:13)? Name some people in the Bible to whom water was a curse. Recall some biblical situations in which water was a blessing. Relate the instances in which Job experiences both the disastrous and the beneficial aspects of storms.
4. Describe your emotions at witnessing a dramatic water rescue (either in real life or on TV). What should be our emotion at seeing someone respond to a gospel invitation to get "saved" from his or her sins? Why is the thrill not always there?

CHAPTER 5: A HOLY BOLDNESS

1. Describe a situation in which you approached someone in a high position boldly yet respectfully. What was the result? When you approach God in worship, in what ways are you bold? How do you make sure you are also respectful?

2. From the following verses describe God: Numbers 23:19; Deuteronomy 4:24,31; 7:9,21; Nehemiah 9:18; Job 37:22,23; Psalm 29:1,2; 42:2; 46:1; 47:7; 65:5; Isaiah 9:6; 40:10,11; Jeremiah 23:23,24; Nahum 1:2; Luke 18:19; John 4:24; Romans 2:11; 11:22; 1 John 1:5. How do you account for such opposing attributes as kindness and sternness, justice and mercy, revenge and love?

3. When Mary Magdalene and "the other Mary" discovered that Jesus had risen from the dead, they were "afraid yet filled with joy" (Matt. 28:8). Relate a time when you experienced similar contrasting emotions.

4. What insights does Hebrews 12:18-29 provide concerning worship? Which ones thrill you most?

CHAPTER 6: A FITTING LIFESTYLE

1. How do you account for the fact that some people who profess to know God have speech patterns and/or lifestyles that are not honoring to His name? What measures can we take to keep our lives above reproach?

2. When you think of God's Spirit as Someone who lives inside of you (your Houseguest), how do you feel? Relate a time when you disappointed Him. A time when you probably made Him smile.

3. Divide a piece of paper into two columns. Mark them "What Displeases God" and "What Pleases God." Read Ephesians 4:17—5:20, filling in the columns as you read. In which of these behavioral areas have you moved from Displeasing to Pleasing? What area would you like the Holy Spirit to touch next?

4. Read Hebrews 12:4-11. Why does God discipline us? What kinds of discipline might He use? Name at least three good things discipline can produce.

CHAPTER 7: COVERING THE FEET (OUR CHRISTIAN WALK)

1. Describe a time when you came to a point beyond which you weren't sure you should go. Which of these instructions did you follow: STOP, LOOK, LISTEN, GO? What was the outcome? If you

had it to do over again, what would you change?

2. How is the Christian advised to walk in Psalm 1:1,2; 89:15; Proverbs 13:20; Jeremiah 6:16; Micah 6:8; 2 John 6? What attitudes prevent us from obeying these admonitions?

3. What do you consider hindrances to moving forward in your Christian experience? How do you think God views these road-blocks? What do you think He wants you to do about them?

4. Why do people fear the future? As you look forward to the new millennium, do you feel confident or afraid? Why? How does trust in the Lord Jesus Christ affect one's view of what lies ahead?

CHAPTER 8: COVERING THE KNEES (OUR PRAYER LIFE)

1. For what do you thank God regularly? What petitions do you make? Give an example of a time when you were pleasantly surprised by the answer to a prayer. Of a time when you were disappointed.

2. Read Philippians 1:9,10, inserting a loved one's name in place of *your* and *you*. Read John 17:9, substituting the names of children for *them*, *those* and *they*. Read the rest of the chapter to see if you want to personalize other phrases.

3. What happened when the following people prayed: Hannah (1 Sam. 1:27); Elijah (1 Kings 18:36-38); Hezekiah (2 Kings 20:1-6); David (Ps. 32:5); Daniel (6:6-23); Jonah (2—4); Paul (2 Cor. 12:7-9)? What can we learn from these examples?

4. In Romans 8:18-27, we read about "groaning." For what is the whole creation groaning? We ourselves? When the Holy Spirit groans in prayer on our behalf, of what can we be certain? How does this make you feel?

CHAPTER 9: UP TO THE WAIST (REPRODUCING OUR FAITH)

1. Describe "the perfect witnessing situation." How would it start? How would it progress? How would it end? Why are our attempts to share our faith less than perfect?

2. Compare a time when you shared your faith by relying on the Holy Spirit's leading with a time when you relied on your own persuasiveness. What emotions do you experience when you realize it is the Holy Spirit's job to save souls; it is our job to witness to our faith?

3. Read John 4:1-42. Why did Jesus "have" to go through racially tense Samaria? How did He initiate a conversation with the woman at the well? How did He turn the conversation to spiritual things? What

was the woman's reaction? How did Jesus handle her diversionary tactics? What lessons can we learn from Jesus' example?

4. On a sheet of paper list some of the reasons Christians don't share their faith more frequently. What is your biggest hindrance? What can you do to remove this roadblock to progress?

CHAPTER 10: ENVELOPING THE HEART
(OUR HIDDEN DESIRES)

1. Think of a heart patient you know personally. What caused the patient to seek medical help? What was the diagnosis? What treatment was prescribed? What was the outcome? How is the patient maintaining health? Draw some spiritual parallels. For all who receive new "hearts," what is God's promise in regard to longevity (1 John 2:17)?

2. Read Isaiah 59:1-3, noting the parts of the body tainted by sin. What relationship does the heart have to the other parts of the body (v. 13)? What is God's solution to a sinful heart (see Ezek. 36:26)? What goes along with the gift of a new heart?

3. When one receives a heart to know God, what changes are obvious? Which change is the most precious to you? Why?

4. As we proceed through life, what questions could we ask ourselves to make sure our motives, intentions, passions and desires are pure in the sight of God?

CHAPTER 11: OVER THE HEAD
(OUR CONTROL CENTER)? NO!

1. Describe your first experience of putting your face in the water. How did you feel when you realized you couldn't breathe? What helped you get over your fear of water? Draw some spiritual parallels.

2. What does Samuel Shoemaker mean by, "There is a death to self in coming into the stream of the Spirit"? What makes this "death" hard? Why?

3. Read Philippians 2:1-11. How do verses 1-4 speak to interpersonal relationships? What does it mean to have "the same attitude as Christ Jesus" (v. 5)? How would you chart the Christian experience as it progresses from before knowing Christ to the new birth to arriving in heaven?

4. As we are caught up in the routine of each day, what are some things that keep us from hearing the Spirit's voice? From building each other up by speaking encouraging words? From reading the Bible?

From humbling ourselves to serve others? What can we do to overcome these obstacles?

CHAPTER 12: SURRENDER! WHAT IF I CAN'T?

1. What images come to mind when you hear the word "surrender"?
   When is it wise to surrender? Unwise? Describe a time when you
   failed to surrender (give in) and later wish you had.
2. What does Marguerite Reiss mean when she asks, "Why must you
   wait until you can do it before you do it"?
3. Do you agree with John Powell that it is not, "If God shows us, we
   will believe," but rather, "If we believe, God will show us"? How
   about with Dietrich Bonhoeffer that it is not, "Once we believe, we
   will obey," but rather, "Unless we obey, we cannot believe"? If these
   two authors are correct, the order of events involved in the new
   birth would be (1) obedience, (2) belief and (3) proof. Do you agree?
   What other things happen as well? Where do they fit in?
4. Read Romans 7:14-25. What inner conflict does Paul describe? What
   does he blame for his inability to win the "war"? Who does he say
   will rescue him?

CHAPTER 13: WHERE DO I GO FOR HELP?

1. Describe a time when you tried to fix something yourself and later
   had to call in an expert. How did you feel? What did the expert say?
2. Read Psalm 139:1-18, listing the Holy Spirit's qualifications for being
   an expert Helper in times of need. Which qualifications bring you
   the most comfort? Why?
3. What emotions are involved when someone comes into an inheritance? What challenges lie ahead? What help does one need?
4. Read Galatians 2:20. What does it mean to be "crucified with
   Christ"? What does the use of the present perfect tense ("have been
   crucified") tell you? Now read Philippians 3:10. How would you
   restate Paul's desire? According to this verse, what must precede our
   receiving "the power of Christ's resurrection"? Does the teaching
   about being identified with Christ's suffering and death disturb you
   or bring you comfort? Why?

CHAPTER 14: HERE GOES! I'M TAKING THE PLUNGE

1. What do people mean when they talk about "taking the plunge"?
   Describe a time when you "took a plunge." What were your feelings

right before you did it? Right after? How did your venture turn out?

2. What does C. S. Lewis mean when he says, "It is easy for those who do it"?

3. On a sheet of paper make three columns. In the first column list the following verbs: *commit, lean, rest, surrender, yield, abandon, trust* and *wait.* In the second column write what each verb requires us to do before we can enjoy its benefits. In the third column state what God does as a result.

4. Read Joshua 3 and 4. What instructions were given to the people? To the priests? What miracle took place? Compare and contrast this miracle to the one at the Red Sea (see Exod. 14). After the people crossed over the Jordan, what were they told to do? What was the purpose of these stones? What memorials might be appropriate to mark the yielding of one's life to God?

CHAPTER 15: FROM A TRICKLE TO A TORRENT

1. Reread the first six paragraphs of chapter 15. Think of the "river" as your experience with Christianity. Restate the ideas in each paragraph keeping that in mind, mentioning your spiritual beginnings, the progression of your faith over time, times of overexuberance and God's ultimate control. Do the same with your church. Then with *the* Church.

2. Describe a time when you were "carried along" by the current of a new idea, a movement or a force. Was it a good or bad experience? Why?

3. Share a time when the Holy Spirit quenched your thirst, cleansed you from sin, revealed your true self, taught you a thrilling truth, became a source of enjoyment, gave you a sense of belonging or inspired you.

4. Read 1 Corinthians 12. What truth concerning the bestowal of "spiritual gifts" (abilities given by the Spirit) is mentioned three times in verses 4-6? What is the purpose of these gifts? Who determines who gets what? What percentage of Christians have been "baptized" into Christ's Body? To what extent is love important in implementing spiritual gifts (see 1 Cor. 13)?

CHAPTER 16: TREASURES IN THE SAND

1. Describe a time you found a "treasure." Did you get more satisfaction out of the hunt or the find? Why?

2. According to Colossians 2:2,3, where do the treasures of wisdom and

knowledge lie? According to Isaiah 33:5,6, what is the key to unlocking God's "treasure chest"? Why is this the key?

3. Share a Scripture verse that "leaped off the page and into your life." What was the result?

4. When Matthew talks about praying for "bread" and not receiving a "stone" (7:9-12), what is he trying to communicate? What should be our attitude when God answers contrary to our expectations?

CHAPTER 17: FULL NETS

1. Describe a time when you watched fisherfolk react to a good catch. How did you as a spectator react?

2. What risks do we take every time we share our faith? What are the rewards? How can we minimize the risks and increase the rewards?

3. Read Acts 1:1-11. To be effective in outreach, of what do we have to be convinced (see v. 3)? Why is this important? Who is an essential participant in outreach (see v. 5)? Where does Jesus tell His disciples to share their faith? What wisdom do you see in the progression? Where is your "Jerusalem"? How are you doing there? Does God have a prerequisite for foreign ministry (see v. 8)? For large group ministry (see Matt. 25:21)?

4. Samuel Shoemaker divides Christians into four categories: "Some Christians are close to God but remote from people. Some are close to people, but remote from God. Some are close to neither; and some are close to both. Of these last come the real 'fishers of men.'" Into which category do you place yourself? What changes do you need to make to become a better "fisher of men"?

CHAPTER 18: FRUIT FOR ALL SEASONS

1. What is your favorite fruit? Tell why you like it. Have you ever bitten into a fruit that didn't meet your expectations? How did you feel? How did you react to your next bite of fruit? Is there a spiritual lesson here? What is it?

2. Read Galatians 5:16-26. List "the fruit of the Spirit." Which fruit would you like to have more of? According to verse 17, what keeps us from producing fruit? How can we get victory?

3. Examine each fruit of the Spirit and describe the difference between the counterfeit and the genuine (that which the world exhibits and that which the Holy Spirit produces).

4. Read John 15:1-8. What happens to branches that do not produce fruit?

To branches that do produce fruit? How does God "prune" His "branches"? What is the purpose of His pruning? What is the secret to producing fruit (see v. 4)? What does this secret require us to do (see v. 7)?

CHAPTER 19: NO MORE BITTERNESS

1. What good, if any, can come from remembering the hurtful actions of others? When is it time to put them behind us? To what extent does our forgiveness depend on the offender's apology? Who is set free by the act of forgiveness?

2. Note the action words the Bible uses to depict God's forgiveness of our sins: Psalm 32:1; 103:12; Isaiah 1:18; 6:7; 43:25; 44:22; Jeremiah 31:34; Micah 7:18,19; John 1:29; Hebrews 9:26; 1 John 1:9. Which images bless you most? Why?

3. What does the forgiveness of sins require (see Heb. 9:22)? Who shed His blood that we might receive pardon (see 1 Pet. 1:19)? Do you see parallels between what Christ did for us on calvary and what we are expected to do toward those who offend us (see 1 Pet. 2:21-25)?

4. On a piece of paper write down an offense you have forgiven but still causes you pain. Now crumble the paper and set fire to it. When you are tempted to nurse the hurt, remember you have relinquished it to God.

CHAPTER 20: A HEALING TOUCH

1. Describe a time when you prayed for a miracle. Did it come? What effect did the outcome have on your faith? What if the outcome had been different?

2. According to the following verses, upon what should our faith be based (or not based): John 20:29-31; Romans 10:17; 1 Corinthians 1:22-24?

3. According to Matthew 8:16, how many people did Jesus heal? Matthew 14:36? 20:29-34? Mark 10:46-52? Luke 7:21? What impression do you get from Luke 5:15,16? John 11:6,21,37? Was the sick one's faith a contributing factor in Matthew 9:2? 9:22? Luke 8:26-39? What conclusions can you draw?

4. When faced with your impending death or that of a loved one, what things in life become important? What fades in importance? What brings comfort? What emotions are stirred when you read John's vision of heaven (see Rev. 21:1-4)? Read aloud the last invitation in the Bible, one that involves water. What, my friend, is your response?

Learn to Fight On Your Knees

THE PRAYER WARRIOR SERIES
from C. Peter Wagner

Warfare Prayer
A biblical and factual guide that will help erase your fears and doubts, leading you to new levels of prayer.
Paperback ISBN 08307.15134 • $10.99
Video SPCN 85116.00612 • $29.99

Prayer Shield
A powerful tool to help organize and mobilize intercessors in the church, providing a defense for the pastor against satanic attacks.
Paperback ISBN 08307.15142 • $10.99
Video SPCN 85116.00620 • $29.99

Breaking Strongholds In Your City
Identify the enemy's territory in your city, focus your prayers and take back your neighborhoods for God.
Paperback ISBN 08307.16386 • $10.99
Video SPCN 85116.00647 • $29.99

Churches That Pray
Examine what prayer is, how prayer builds the local church and how prayer can break down the walls between the church and the community.
Paperback ISBN 08307.16580 • $10.99
Video SPCN 85116.00639 • $29.99

Confronting the Powers
Learn how Jesus and the early church practiced spiritual warfare and what we can learn from their example.
Hardcover ISBN 08307.18192 • $16.99

The Prayer & Spiritual Warfare Video Series
Each tape in this powerful video seminar series features teachings from two respected leaders in the growing prayer movement as they reveal God's vision for today's Church.

Volume 1
Harold Caballeros
Spiritual Warfare
John Eckhardt
Deliverance: Our Spiritual Weapon
Video • UPC 607135.002499 • $19.99

Volume 2
John Dawson
Breaking Strongholds Through Reconciliation
Alice Smith
Intimacy with God
Video • UPC 607135.002536 • $19.99

Volume 3
Cindy Jacobs
Prophetic Intercession
Ted Haggard
Intercessors in the Church
Video • UPC 607135.002505 • $19.99

Volume 4
Jack Deere
The Conspiracy Against the Supernatural
Ed Silvoso
Prayer Evangelism
Video • UPC 607135.001935 • $19.99

Volume 5
Francis Frangipane
Soldiers of the Cross
Ed Silvoso
Doing Greater Works Than Jesus
Video • UPC 607135.002512 • $19.99

Volume 6
James Marocco
Binding and Loosing
Eddie Smith
The Basics of Deliverance
Video • UPC 607135.002529 • $19.99

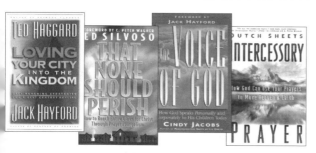

Loving Your City Into the Kingdom
Ted Haggard and Jack Hayford
Practical, city-reaching strategies for a 21st century revival. Ground-breaking articles from Christian leaders who are witnessing an amazing outpouring of God's love on their communities. Also available as a video seminar featuring Ted Haggard.
Hardcover ISBN 08307.18737 • $17.99
Video (Haggard) UPC 607135-001119 • $39.99

That None Should Perish
Ed Silvoso
Learn the powerful principles of "prayer evangelism" and how you can join with others to bring the gospel to your community.
Paperback ISBN 08307.16904 • $10.99

The Voice of God
Cindy Jacobs
God still speaks to His Church today. This book cuts through the confusion to show how the gift of prophecy can and should be used to edify contemporary churches.
Paperback ISBN 08307.17730 • $10.99
Video UPC 607135-001195 • $39.99
(Available May '97)

Intercessory Prayer
Dutch Sheets
Discover how your prayers can move heaven and earth. Learn the biblical dynamics of intercession and invigorate your prayer life.
Hardcover ISBN 08307.18885 • $16.99

Available at your local Christian Bookstore